The
Greatest
Networkers
in the World

The Greatest Networkers in the World
from Youngevity

John Milton Fogg

Published by YGY Press
2400 Boswell Road
Chula Vista, CA 91914

YoungevitysGreatestNetworkers.com

ISBN: 978-0-9907171-0-2

BUSINESS & ECONOMICS / Marketing / Direct
SELF-HELP / Personal Growth / Success

Table of Contents

Introduction

I once wrote a book...

The Greatest Networker in the World told the inspirational story of a young man on the brink of quitting Network Marketing, and the mentor who helped him turn his life around in one remarkable weekend.

Having sold more than a million copies, it's among the most well-known books in Network Marketing and many people have told me it changed their lives "for the better forever."

That book was fiction.

This book is different. It's all true.

You're about to meet and get to know, however briefly, some real-life *Greatest Networkers in the World*. The unexpected thing is, they are all in the same company. Youngevity.

They are indeed "ordinary people:" A single mom, struggling financially, a plumber deeply in debt, a hugely successful thoroughly disenchanted dentist, the Chief Financial Officer of a $1.5 billion Network Marketing company with something to prove, a Taco Bell manager with no self-esteem... All in all a select collection of men and women, each with their own unique personal and professional challenges, who overcame them to achieve lifestyles of Health, Time and Money they once could only distantly dream of. And today, together, they're helping thousands of people just like you and me to do the same.

I could have joined any Network Marketing company. I chose Youngevity. These people are the reason I did.

Enjoy the book.

Thanks & God Bless.

— John

90 For Life

William Andreoli is the President of Youngevity — and he's also a Renaissance Entrepreneur.

Bill started his first restaurant at age 18. Over time he's owned and operated as many as six of them — all successful — and he's still a restaurant owner today.

And Bill's also had very successful (part-time) careers in real estate, stock market investing, as a Network Marketing distributor and field leader, and he founded and ran his own Networking Company, Financial Destination Inc. (FDI).

"I started FDI," Bill said, "because I saw how many people were struggling financially, and how hungry they were to learn about making and managing money."

They say, *It Takes Money to Make Money.* "That's true," Bill says, "but most people can't even *afford* to learn what it takes to make money, so they're stopped before they start."

> **Bill saw that all these people wanted the same information he did. The difference was, he could afford to get it. They couldn't.**

"I was going to a number of *No Money Down* real estate and *Make Money in the Stock Market* seminars around Boston and Concord, New Hampshire — like the ones you see advertised on late-night infomercials. The people in the audience didn't realize they were really attending a three-hour *commercial*, trying to sell them on an expensive weekend workshop. More than 500 people would show up, but only about 10 of us had the $4000 or $8000 to sign up."

That challenged Bill's entrepreneurial mind and he started asking some important questions:

"What if we created a company where we gave them the education they really needed to make money? We teach them about real estate and the stock market. And we'll also provide services like credit restoration and debt elimination, where we're actually doing the work to help them."

He also asked: "What if we tied that on to a membership that they could afford? No big out of pocket money. Not $5,000 or $10,000. Maybe they're spending $50 a month, and they're getting the kind of practical, useful information they can apply plus hands on support."

"And what if when they told a few people who joined them they'd make money? At the least, their membership could be free and they are not paying anything at all."

Bill put the answers to his questions together, which quickly turned into FDI, the premier Financial Services and Lifestyle Benefits Company that he started in 2003. It's no surprise that it took off right away.

Bill ran FDI for nine years - until merging with Youngevity.

"One of the leaders with FDI connected with one of the leaders of Youngevity," Bill said, "and they believed our two companies would be a great partnership. So, one day I found myself on a conference call with them and Steve Wallach (CEO of Youngevity)."

"I didn't know Steve, but I knew about his father, Dr. Joel Wallach, from when I was 19 years old, and working with another health and wellness company. We'd all heard of *Dead Doctors Don't Lie*. But I knew nothing about Youngevity as a company."

On that call, Bill and Steve simply "talked shop," sharing their experiences in the field and running their respective companies. There was no real outcome per se, except that Steve and Bill developed a healthy respect and appreciation for each other and started a professional friendship.

"Every time I'd be going out West, and the Youngevity folks knew about it, they'd suggest we get together," Bill said. "We finally met face-to-face at the Hotel Del Coronado in San Diego. Soon after that, my wife and I went to their corporate office in Chula Vista, California. We had a great meeting and over the next few months we kept in touch frequently."

It wasn't until Bill saw Doc Wallach in person that his wheels began to turn. Bill thought, "This isn't some 'Me Too' company! This is the Original."

"If I was going to do something with another company, it would have to be something that's much bigger than what we were already doing," Bill said. "And Doc's message was that big."

And once Bill started drilling down into Youngevity, he started saying, "Man, they've got it going on. They've got the message. They've got the product. They've got the celebrity, the icon, the rock star, the legend... in Doc."

Bill knew Youngevity could be the next billion dollar company. A *Legacy* company. And was sure he and his people could help.

"We finally made the decision in August of 2011," Bill said. We had our final FDI convention, and we had invited the Wallach's, and Doc, and a number of Youngevity leaders. We introduced Youngevity, and had Doc on stage and he rocked it like he always does."

So Bill Andreoli of FDI, and Steve Wallach of Youngevity joined forces. "We called it the perfect storm - or *better*, the perfect marriage," Bill said, "Steve and myself, we do have our own personalities and talents. For instance, one of Steve's is obviously product development and one of mine is in the marketing."

"Within a few months of us being together, we saw that they had a powerful message and superior products, but (even) though Doc was a big piece, you didn't get one unified message."

As a marketer, Bill knew that a simple and unified message was something Youngevity must have in order to become a billion-dollar legacy company. So that's what he focused in on.

"Right after Thanksgiving, I was trying to come up with something that would identify who Youngevity is and what Doc is really all about. I was going to see Doc where ever he was, as many times as I could. What I saw right away was people always asked him the same questions— and he always gave them the same answers; again and again and again."

"They asked, 'Who needs to be on this stuff?' And Doc would reply, 'If you can fog a mirror, you need these 90 essential nutrients.' No pulled punches with that one," Bill said. "That's pretty blunt, very direct, and obviously *not* a marketing message that I'd go put on bill boards."

"And then people would ask, 'How long do I need to be on this stuff?' And Doc would ask them in return, 'How long do you need oxygen?' And again," Bill said, "true, but a bit harsh for a marketing message."

viii

Two things stuck with Bill: The 90 essential nutrients were required; non-negotiable for Doc. And not for just weeks or months. Not even for a few years. Doc was talking about taking them *For Life!*

If you can fog a mirror... As long as you need oxygen. What Doc was saying came down to three words, 90 FOR LIFE.

"That was it," Bill said, "That's what I was looking for."

Bill phoned Doc right away and asked his opinion. "What do I think?" he replied "You've summarized my 40 years in three words. I love it. When can I use it?" And he's been saying it ever since.

"In the first 10 months with 90 For Life, we had 300% growth," Bill said. "Which is pretty unbelievable. And (now, two years later,) we are on our eighth consecutive record-breaking month. And the message hasn't changed."

"Our English word *slogan*, comes from the Scotch-Galic, *slaughgharim*," Bill explained. "It means 'battle cry.' With *90 For Life*, the people of Youngevity are leading the charge to become a billion-dollar legacy company."

Bill Andreoli, lives in Windham, New Hampshire, where Youngevity's executive offices are located, with his wife Duyen and their children Kylee, who's 14, Parker, who's 13, and Kiana who's 9.

The
Greatest
Networkers...

Consistently Consistent

Dr. Luis Arriaza's parents emigrated from El Salvador to what his mother once described as "one of the most beautiful parts of sunny Southern California— South Central Los Angeles." If you're familiar with California, then you know South Central L.A. is not quite a resort area. Home to the infamous gangs the Bloods & the Crips, in most all ways it's the absolute opposite.

The Ariazza's purpose for coming to America was because they desperately wanted a better life for their children. One day while walking in downtown Los Angeles, Luis' mother came across a tall, handsome, American man with blond hair and blue eyes and asked him in her very broken English, "What is the secret to success in America?"

The man told her that the secret was education. Even though he was a complete stranger, she believed him, and that became the foundation for Luis' early life— for his entire life.

"What my parents lacked in formal education," Luis said, "they made up for in tremendous faith."

> **"They pushed us, they motivated us, even punished us. They did whatever they needed to do to make sure that we went to school. At a very young age, I learned to love to learn."**

When Luis was 15 years old he thought that he was going to be an attorney. He attended a career day at his school and... "This attorney showed up," Luis said. "He was late. He was out of shape. He had a huge stain on his red polyester tie. He told us how

1

he had flunked the Bar seven times. By the end of his story I was underneath my chair thinking, "Hey if this is what I have to look forward to... No thank you!'"

Luis came home pretty disappointed, but his mom said, "Let's go see a doctor."

Luis already had enough for one day and said no, but his mother insisted, "No, we are going to the chiropractor." Luis didn't even know what a chiropractor was.

They sat in a very humble Latino South Central LA chiropractic office and Luis watched the people come and go.

"Some walked in limping. Some people came in bent this way and twisted that. Others had to be pushed in or even carried," Luis said. "But I saw almost every individual that came in walk out different. Not only was there a positive physical change, but there was an emotional difference, too. There was a spiritual shift and I could feel it. These people *really were different!*"

Right then Luis had a revelation. "If I can help people feel the way this doctor makes them feel, I want to do this for the rest of my life."

That summer, Luis volunteered at the doctor's office. Eventually he went to chiropractic school and became the youngest student ever to graduate the program.

Luis had just turned 24 years old. He was a licensed chiropractor done with his academic schooling. But he was broke. He still didn't have two pennies to rub together and now he had these massive college loans to pay.

Dr. Luis Arriaza

Luis told himself, "I don't know how to be chiropractor. I'm not a business man. I don't have a reference for making a lot of money. I don't even have a reference for being a business owner." But he knew someone who did.

"I'd met a chiropractor at a seminar," Luis said, "I felt like this man was going to be the bridge from where I was to where I wanted to be. After the seminar I went up to him and said, 'Could you be my mentor? Could you coach me, because I'm willing to do whatever it takes— as long as it's ethical and legal— to be a successful chiropractor?' He said, 'Absolutely, give me a call.'"

Luis called him that following Monday, but the doctor didn't take his call. Luis called him the week after that, but he didn't take that call.

Luis called him for six months straight. The man never answered nor returned Luis' calls.

Finally, after almost seven months, Luis' office phone rang and it was the chiropractor. Luis was super-excited when the doctor said, "Okay, we are going to start the coaching." Luis asked, "Doc, with all due respect, I've been calling you faithfully every week for seven months, why didn't you ever call me back?" And the doctor replied, "Because I only work with people who will do whatever it takes to succeed. I know that if you were going to be disappointed, if you were going to be sad or depressed or you were going to feel bad because I didn't call you back, then you're not the person I want to coach. Not the person that's really willing to pay the price of success."

Great lesson. And Luis learned another important lesson, too:

Determination will win over any other skill or ability.

3

"And so he proceeded to coach me," Luis said. "He gave me the principle, he gave me the philosophy, he gave me our universal premise."

At the end of that first year, Luis was averaging about 180 patients a day. At the end of three years, Luis and his wife Evelia had seven healthy and successful practices.

Luis had found his calling. He earned his first million by the age of 27. He didn't do any advertising. No internet marketing. Luis built his practices the same way he builds his Network Marketing business today — person-to-person.

"My mentor taught me how to build relationships with my patients," Luis said.

"He taught me how to be real with my patients, how to listen and how to seek to understand before being understood.

He showed me how to learn what they were looking for instead of what I wanted them to have."

"All I would do was teach my patients the philosophy of chiropractic by telling the story. I would spend over an hour of real personal connection time with my patients and the practices just grew and grew and grew."

With all of the experience Luis had speaking with his patients, he and his wife, Evelia, soon started doing seminars; first for chiropractors, then that evolved into doing seminars for the public as well.

Through a friend of his wife, Luis was invited to speak at the Dept. of Social Services Goals Program. He had no idea he'd be on stage with *Chicken Soup for the Soul* author Mark Victor Hansen. Nor did he have a clue there'd be close to a thousand people in the audience.

"I was petrified," Luis said. "I dragged Evelia into the restroom and I told her 'I don't know if I can do this.' She said, 'Since God has given you this opportunity and the ability you've just got to go out there and show up. You know you can do it. Just step-up!'"

Luis did his hour–and-a-half presentation and everybody loved it!

Eventually, he and Evelia created a professional speaking company called "Soul-to-Soul." They were having seminars of up to a thousand people, four to five times a year and they also put together an on-going coaching program. Business was booming!

"I was doing a coaching session at a hotel in Baldwin Park (not the classiest part of town)," Luis said, "and I saw this beautiful Bentley parked outside. I immediately went back into the hotel and asked, 'Who owns that car?'"

"They directed me to a meeting that the owner of the Bentley was giving. I sat in the back and listened. I was 30 or 31 years old at the time, but I had never heard of Network Marketing before."

"I'd read a study once," Luis recalled, "that said the average person will have four God given ideas in their lifetime, which when acted upon would make them wealthy."

"Most people never act on these inspired thoughts. This was one of mine," Luis said, "and I acted."

When the meeting ended, Luis walked up and gave the speaker his card. The owner of the Bentley was also the owner of the Network

Marketing Company. He sat down with Luis for an hour-long conversation that lasted nearly four hours.

"I fell in love with the concept," Luis said. "I fell in love with the thought that the only way that you grow is by first helping other people grow — and the bigger you help other people grow then the bigger your dream becomes."

Luis first check was $57. But he did the same thing he'd done in chiropractic: He found the best Network Marketer he could and told him, "Tell me exactly what you do and I'll do it — as long as it's ethical and legal. I am coachable. I won't change a thing."

His mentor-to-be told Luis that lots of people had said that to him, but they all ended up doing something different. And then they would come back and blame him for their failure.

Luis said, "Well, I'm not them. I *am* coachable. Tell me exactly what to do. I don't know Network Marketing, but I want to learn *and* I'm willing to pay the price." So he gave Luis the first few steps — as much to test him as anything else. And Luis did indeed do everything he was told. After a year, Luis' income was more than $115,000 a month and he was the fastest growing Latino in that company. Those very same steps Luis used then, he does — and teaches his people to do — in his business today.

"The goal of Network Marketing for us," Luis said, "is not to create an organization, but to create a culture— and all cultures depend on a core philosophy."

"Our philosophy is one of hope and inspiration based on universal principles that once people learn and apply, it's nearly impossible for them not to change and grow and succeed. "

"The key to success in Network Marketing," Luis said, "is consistency. Staying in the game. After a year or two, even average people can match the income of their full-time job. Being consistently consistent outweighs talent and skills."

"If you have a plan and you consistently work the plan every day, you *will* succeed. It never fails."

"I believe we all have a calling. I believe we all have a purpose. I believe that there is nothing more powerful than to see someone's life change with the spoken word." Luis said. "I believe God has given me an opportunity to share a message that changes people's lives; a hope-filled message; a personally transforming message. I find immense joy that we are being used by God in that way. Not just myself, but my wife and my kids... all of us."

"I don't ever clock-in to work," Luis said. "I don't have to answer to anybody. I set my own schedule and I can really do what I'm passionate about— which is leadership and personal transformation— every single day of my life. I mean for me that's the most fascinating... The most rewarding... The most exciting aspect of Network Marketing."

"I know my company will fulfill everything that a person looking to build a Network Marketing organization needs. It will fulfill that and then some. If you just give yourself an opportunity and go to work a little bit you'll see what a great life you can create. And we have so many great people to help you."

Luis and Evelia Arriaza have three children — Fabian 13, Isaiah 7, Elisha 5. They live in Glendora, California, "The Pride of the Foothills," located a "million miles" from South Central L.A.

Love Like Crazy. Then Love More.

Tom and Denice Chenault were born only 30 miles from each other in Colorado. Tom grew up on a small dairy farm south of Denver in Littleton, and Denice grew up in Evergreen, about 17 miles to the west.

Both of Denice's parents were teachers. Her mom taught fourth grade and her dad taught English, some history and was a high school counselor. Denice's dad also had a passion for Plains Indian art and today, he is one of only a handful of experts in the world who restores Native American pieces. Denice and her sister Amy spent many summers following their father to museums from Nebraska to the Dakotas, down to Santa Fe.

Tom was one of four kids and the family were caretakers of the farm where they lived and worked. "From the day I was born," Tom said, "my mom and dad had their hands full with my sister who was beautiful and the star of the show, an older brother who was very ill and a little brother who was a premature baby born weighing only 2-1/2 pounds. So I got virtually no attention, which really kind of shaped who I am today." Plus, the family had no money. "Not poor like poor," Tom said, "but plenty poor."

Denice remembers, even as a little girl of eight or nine years old, wanting to find her passion. She tried ballet, but that wasn't for her.

Then she found horses. She started riding hunter-jumpers and she loved it.

"Evergreen was a fairly wealthy community," Denice said, "so I was competing with girls who were riding $10,000 and $20,000 horses. The horse that I had cost $2,000. So the only way I could

9

compete at that level was to become the best that I could with what I had."

Denice may not have had the greatest horse — hard to do even on a two-teacher income — but she out-practiced the other kids by a huge amount. "And then I had jobs," she said. "I did a lot of babysitting. I packed up the school horses for the riding lessons. I mucked stalls. I braided manes at shows. I did what I could in order to help support my habit."

"When I was 15," Denice said, "I became the Reserve Champion for Colorado in Equitation, which is solely based on how the rider looks on the horse. We went to the Kansas City Royal Horse Show and the only ribbon that came home from our barn was from me. It was the first time in my life that I saw what passion coupled with hard work could get you."

Tom was a really, really good student in grade school in Littleton, Colorado. In high school the teachers kept telling him how smart he was.

"So as a result, I started taking that for granted." Tom said. "It went from how smart I was and how well I was doing, to how much potential Tom's got but doesn't use."

"That ended up kind of being my story in my life. I graduated from high school with really low grades, but high test scores," Tom said, "and I went to college the same way. Drank myself stupid and got kicked out of 4 or 5 colleges with hundreds of class hours and no degrees." Tom found himself out in the world trying to figure out what he was going to do with his life.

When Denice graduated from high school she sold her horses — it was now her sister Amy's turn — and went to the University of

Colorado at Boulder. She was a Communication/Cultural Anthropology major. Denice's first job right out of college was with CareerTrack: at the time a big employer in Boulder that did seminars for businesses. She worked in the publications department selling books and tapes. Then moved to the marketing department and bought and sold mailing lists.

"I took a course called *Understanding Yourself and Others* through the Dreikurs Relationship Center," Denice said.

"It was a transformational experience for me: Locked in the room for three days and what came out— who came out— on the other side was just unbelievable."

Denice took a number of courses, flying down to Austin, Texas every other month for four-day trainings. She did that for two years until she became an instructor.

"I just loved it," Denice said, "because I was able to see such huge transformation. People could just make leaps and bounds of difference in their life in a short amount of time. I taught all over the country. We even taught a course in Jerusalem. That was an amazing experience for me at a very young age." Denice was just 25.

After Tom stopped going to college-after-college, he started running a restaurant. "My boss was an unbelievable taskmaster," he said. "We had 103 employees under the age of 18, and 75,000 people a month going through the doors. It was pandemonium all the time. It really, really taught me all about life, because I learned that hard work paid off big time."

Tom also learned that making connections and being as nice as he could, "not blowing up bridges," was completely *the* most important thing. "I ended up building a rolodex in those days that has carried me through my whole life. I learned how to make people know they were important and that lesson's never ended."

"I finally drank myself out of the restaurant business," Tom said. "I was one of those guys that the restaurants that *could* afford me didn't want me, and the restaurants that *couldn't* afford me... I mean it was just beyond belief. I was a man without a country."

Tom's last name is Chenault, and General Claire Chennault was a famous World War II aviator. So Tom became an airplane salesman based on the cachet of his last name.

"I walked into every office of every person that wanted to buy an airplane,' Tom said. "And the very first thing they said was are you related to Clair Chennault? And I'd say, 'No, but do you want to buy an airplane?" As a result, I did pretty well there."

But airplane buyers were few and far between and even though Tom was working like crazy and flying airplanes all over the country, he wasn't making enough money to feed his family.

So Tom got into the stock brokerage business. And the rest, he says, is history.

"I couldn't see the product," Tom said, "and as an alcoholic and a crazy man, I could make up almost any story around a stock I wanted. Plus there was no limit on the amount of money you could make. I would get paychecks for $50,000 and just be absolutely sobbing. But so many people had gotten decimated by the investments I had put them in, because I was either listening to my greed or I was listening to the brokerage firms telling us to buy stocks that ultimately went down. It was a terrible, terrible hamster cage to be in."

Tom's solution was to drink like crazy, and then drink some more.

"I got two DUI's, which is Driving Under the Influence, and two disturbing the peace arrests, all in one month in 1988. Finally I crawled into Alcoholics Anonymous."

Denice ended up owning the Boulder Center of Understanding Yourself... bringing instructors in and doing courses. This was from about 1988 to 1992. It was a $500 weekend; a lot of money in the late '80s and '90s.

"You had to really go deep with people on the phone," Denice said. "Processing with them, learning what they would like to change and what they would get out of the weekend. I got a little burnt out because I was enrolling one course every month, so it was always 'Okay, how are you going to put 20 new people in the next course?' It just got to be too much for me."

Denice ended up selling her center. She was also pregnant with her son and stayed home being a full-time mother for a couple of years.

In AA they told Tom he had to stop doing what got him drunk in the first place. So Tom, "acting like a maniac," quit his job. A bad move that would eventually be the best decision he'd ever made, but at the time...

"I found myself living in a huge house with no income whatsoever and running around looking for jobs," Tom said.

"No one would hire me at any price, because I was just a hand grenade looking for a place to pull the pin. I was unemployable."

Love Like Crazy. Then Love More.

"I act like I chose Network Marketing," Tom said, "but Network Marketing chose me, because it was the last house on the block."

"There was no credit check. No background check. There was nothing except here's a place where you can go to work right now, work as hard as you want and you might just make some money and be able to feed your family."

Tom and Denice had both gotten divorced — and they both had children. Denice was a single mom raising her son Dominic. Tom lived by himself and saw his children as often as he could.

Denice was dating a guy she had known back when she was married. She knew his ex-wife fairly well, and one day Denice said to her, "You know, he kind of drinks a lot." Her friend said, "Yeah." And *then* she said...

"Maybe you should have a conversation with my boyfriend Tom, because he's been sober for about 10 years now."

"She gave me Tom's number and I called him up," Denice said. "I told him, 'I'd like to talk to you about this guy. Would you be willing to meet me for a cup of coffee?' He said, 'Absolutely.' So we met in Boulder at the Starbucks and Tom basically said, 'You've got to tell this guy that it's either you or the alcohol.'"

Denice thought, "Well that's going to go over well." And sure enough, he chose the alcohol, but in the process Tom and Denice became good friends. They would talk on the phone every now and then. They would meet for lunch or dinner every now and then.

"By that time, I was working as a distributor rep for hair care products," Denice said. "My paycheck was 100% commission, which just scared the daylights out of me because now I was by myself with a two-year old. I was barely managing to get by."

Denice was sending her son Dominic to a private school, which took all she had— and then some. "I had a mortgage on a town home. My car had gotten repossessed, so I was driving my grandmother's Volvo. I didn't have cable because that had gotten turned off, and there were a lot of nights that we had tomato soup and grilled cheese sandwiches for dinner."

Tom called one time and Denice said, "You'd better talk quick," and he said, "Why?" She said because they will shut my phone off any minute. Tom said, "Well, how much is the bill?" Denice told him, "$40." He said, "For God's sakes, give me the number and I'll pay your phone bill."

> **Then Tom said, "Denice, how much do you have in your checking account?" She said, "Funny you should ask."**

"I had one penny in my checkbook," Denice said. "I was so happy because I wasn't overdrawn. So Tom said, 'Let me help you,' and he paid the phone bill. We were very good friends for about three years and I felt awfully strange that he never put a move on me."

Tom thought that Denice thought he was too old. Denice didn't know what Tom thought, but *she* thought it was really strange that he never "put a move" on her. One night they went out to dinner and Denice put a move on Tom. The rest, they both say, is history.

Tom and Denice Chenault were the first distributors to achieve the Ambassador rank in Youngevity. Their respective backgrounds, both personally and professionally, contributed greatly to their success in Network Marketing. Though not always in ways even they expected.

Love Like Crazy. Then Love More.

"There is nothing about my aviation career or my stock brokerage career that had me have any success in Network Marketing," Tom said. "It was quite the opposite."

"Where I got all my experience for Network Marketing was in the restaurant business," Tom said. "The reason I say that is because in the restaurant business you are always serving people. The best product and the best service always won."

"In the brokerage business the scorecard wasn't how much money you made the client. It was how much you made for yourself and the firm. As a result, I had to unlearn that dog-eat-dog mentality."

"I built my career in Network Marketing by basically doing the restaurant business without the restaurant."

"Be as nice as you can to people, work your fingers to the bone but play it like you're not. Let everybody feel like they're the most special person in the world and *mean* it."

Denice's experience leading transformational workshops helped her in being able to connect with people at a deeply personal level, quickly and with ease — for her and for them.

"It's all about finding out who the other person is," Denice said. "Who are they? Are they married? Do they have kids? Do they need help with their house? What do they like to do for fun? What do they want more of in their life? What do they want less of? What's most important to them in their lives?"

Denice and Tom have learned how to effectively marry their differences and optimize their similarities to create a winning partnership in both their marriage and their business.

16

"Tom's up at 5:00 in the morning, asleep by 10:00," Denice said. "I'm awake until midnight and usually get up at about 7:00, 7:30. He's 'hair-on-fire' from 5:00AM to the moment his head hits the pillow. We found a great partnership with each other because a lot of the things that he likes to do, I don't... and a lot of the things I like to do, he doesn't."

One thing the dynamic couple shares is a commitment to their people — to all people. Their motto is:

Love like crazy. Then love more.

"Lots of people are smarter than we are. Lots of people are richer than we are. Lots of people are a lot of things more than we are, but you are going to have a heck of a time out-loving us."

"I know it sounds like a cliché," Tom said. "'The money doesn't matter anymore.' But I am telling you from the bottom of my heart, Denice and I do this business and we will continue to do Youngevity if there isn't a paycheck tied to it, because it's been the greatest thing that ever happened to us."

Tom and Denice Chenault live in Longmont, Colorado. Their daughter Courtney is 25 and lives in Denver. Dominic is 22 and lives in Longmont. And Adrian is 29 and lives in Sydney, Australia with the couple's first grandchildren. Being Chenaults, they fly all around the United States in their classic 1983 Cessna 185 Turbo loving like crazy.

Time Freedom

Maxandra "Max" Desroiser grew up and lived in Port-au-Prince, Haiti, until she was 13 years old. Her parents were divorced, and since her father was more financially stable, the decision was made she would live with him, as he could afford to send her to private school. He had built a jewelry business that started on a street corner, but from there grew into his own shop. Max was even able to earn an allowance working for him.

During the summer, when Max was 12 years old, her world completely crumbled. She had moved back in to stay with her mother, which meant times were a little leaner. One fateful day, her older brothers were coming to pick her up from a party, but never arrived. On their way, they were viciously murdered by a Haitian street gang, becoming victims of the political turmoil that was sweeping the island nation in the early 1990s.

Max stayed with her mother for another year of fear, when finally her mom decided it would be safer for her if she went to live with her uncle in the United States. She told Max it was just a vacation. It wasn't.

A week and a-half after Max arrived in the States, her mom called and told her she wasn't coming back to Haiti.

On Max's 14th birthday, her half-sister came to pick her up to spend just the night - then bring her back the next day - but Max's uncle had other plans. "Keep her," he said. "I don't want to take care of another child."

Time Freedom

For the next three years, Max lived with her sister, a struggling single mom. Max got busy, and even though she didn't speak a word of English when she arrived in America, she was able to graduate from high school a full-year early. By age 16, she was out in the world, on her own and alone.

"I'd gotten a scholarship," Max said. "But they told me they couldn't honor it, because I was an 'out-of-state' student. I didn't have the money, so I went to work instead."

Max had a friend who worked for a mortgage company and she introduced her to the owner who said, "I don't have anything available right now, but you can do marketing for me at night." Max said, "Great!"

"I didn't have a car. I would apply with a lot of temp agencies and I go anywhere they sent me," Max said. "Take the bus. Take the train. A friend of mine who didn't have family here had an apartment, so I moved in with her." They bought an old couch from one of the neighbors and that's where she slept.

Every day she took the bus and went to do her jobs. Then went to school and at night she did marketing at the mortgage company.

"I would sit there and make calls," Max said. "They would pay me $15 when the deal closed." The brokers charged between $3000 and $7000, but that $15 meant so much to Max that she didn't complain. "I was always eager to learn. It didn't matter if I had to sit there and eat my peanut butter and jelly (which I did, day after night). God always provided for me."

"We had our struggles in Haiti, but at the time my father did his best," Max said. "I had a very good life growing up and I've seen

20

both sides of the coin. So when I came here... having to go through the struggles, I just went through them."

One night Max got a call from the owner of the mortgage company she worked for, "Max a position opened during the day and I can pay you $7 an hour." Max had given him her word that when the time came, she'd work for him, so she quit the other company where she was earning $12 an hour and went to work for the mortgage company. Max had her eyes set on becoming a mortgage broker herself.

Within a few months Max became his office manager (with a raise of about a quarter an hour). She kept saying, "I know I can be a broker," but her boss kept saying, "No, you can't."

One day the company's entire group of top producers decided they were going to open an office of their own, and left. The owner said, "Okay, Max, I want you on the floor today." Max was just a few months shy of 18 years old.

Max was going to mortgage school when one of her banking contacts took her aside. "Max," he said, "I'm going to a Tony Robbins seminar this weekend. I think you should come." It would take a lot of money, her entire savings, but Max went anyway.

"My eyes opened wide," Max said. "I realized I didn't have to focus on my struggles. I could focus on moving forward, creating my future, what I really wanted— and I learned I had the power to do that. Didn't matter that people looked at me as this young Haitian girl who hardly spoke English. They didn't see the potential in me. But I did. I left that seminar on top of the world. I was so motivated and fired up! That was the best investment I ever made."

Within months, Max became a top producer. In two years, she opened

her own mortgage company.

Maxandra was just 20 years old.

Most people expected her to go to the "La Petite Haïti" section of the city to open her new mortgage company – But that's not Max. She went straight to Brickell Avenue in downtown Miami, the heart of the financial district. The offices to the left and right of hers were brokering big commercial deals worth millions and millions of dollars. Max said, "Okay, if I'm really going to the top, I need to be around these people. I need to stretch myself." So, she did. Both.

"My company did very well," Max said. "Very, very well. Because of that, I was able to share my success. My sisters came here. I brought my mom up. I was able to give back to them, and also help many young people who worked for me to become brokers."

Just before the 2008 mortgage collapse, Max closed her doors. But it wasn't because of the financial crisis. "Things were becoming just too big," Max said. "I would be at my office from 7:00 in the morning and sometimes I wouldn't leave until 1:00 or 2:00 the next afternoon." Max was exhausted. Running on fumes.

"I was so busy that in the morning, I didn't have time to just kneel down and pray. I came home so tired, I didn't make time to give thanks. I knew the core of my foundation was crumbling," Max said. " Balance just wasn't there – and it wasn't there for years!"

"I didn't have time to spend with my family. Although I was making a lot of money, I didn't have time for the people and things that brought me success."

For that reason, Max believed it was time to move on. The mortgage crisis gave her the opportunity to walk away. To everyone else it didn't make sense. She was doing so well. But Max knew... It was time.

"At first, I did nothing," Max said. "Just stayed still. I prayed, I prayed and I prayed. I didn't realize how tired I was. I didn't see how drained I was. So I prayed. I said, 'God, I want you to just give me a new direction. Whatever it is, I want to use all these experiences I've had to help others.'"

Almost one year later, Max got an email from a friend she hadn't heard from in years. He was in the real estate business. It said, "Max, you have to call me." Max called and he said "Listen, I have something here that I think you should take a look at."

It was FDI, Financial Destination Inc., and Max's friend was Andre Vaughn, the top income earner in the company - although he didn't tell Max.

"So I looked," Max said. She told herself, "This is something I can work with, helping others build their own business." Max knew how much it takes to have a business, to have a big overhead of thousands and thousands of dollars. And she knew all too well the stress that comes with that.

Max was fascinated that in FDI you could start a business for only $500 with no overhead and no employees. In about 30 days, she became a Senior Executive Marketing Director with the company. Max won their Road-to-Convention promotion and became IMD of the year. From there on, it was all about growing and building her team.

"I said, 'Okay, Max, you have to learn the system!'" And Max learned. Fast. Her team took off.

"I got the concept," Max said. "I'd paid the price before, so building the business, getting my team members involved, showing them the mission, came very natural for me."

As vital to the success of the individual and the team as the system is— and the skills, strategies, training and tools that go with it— Max knows it takes something more. Much more.

"It takes heart," Max said. "It takes passion. It takes commitment— and more than that it takes love of people."

"This is a business of you loving people. It is a people business. When you operate in love and you truly open your heart to what people want, what your team members want— doesn't matter what they say or how they are— you just keep moving forward with love."

"I really do believe with that in place, it's just a matter of time. If your dream is to become a million-dollar earner, you will make it. You will absolutely make it! That's what I did," Max said. "I truly opened my heart to my team members and that has absolutely opened another world for me."

What kind of world? The most important world of all for Max: A world of time freedom.

"I know what it is to have a business and be there for 15 hours a day," Max said. "When I was 18 years old I had a goal of where I wanted to live. Two years later, I own a condo right there. Right on the ocean. A beautiful place. But I was never there to enjoy it."

"People say, 'Oh you have these beautiful cars,' but guess what? I didn't drive them. I was always at work. I have a family I didn't have time to see. My mom lived an hour away, but I never had time to be with her, because I was always working."

"Time is so valuable for me," Max said. "For me to be able to do this from my home gives me time freedom."

"A week ago I just felt so grateful. I realized, 'God you answered my prayer. You gave me something I can do where I can touch other people and also serve you.'"

"And I'm doing just that," Max said. "I'm so grateful to have time freedom to be with my little cousin and help teach him and mold him and show him how to grow as a little man. I can spend time with my sisters. I can spend time with my mother."

"God gave me time."

"I believe my purpose is to share my life with others in an enriching way," Max said. "Youngevity empowers me to do that. I love what this company stands for: To transform the mental, emotional, spiritual and financial growth of individuals and businesses around the world."

Maxandra Desroiser lives in Miami, Florida, where she now has time to drive her Lexus whenever she wants, which means when she's not hiking, sky diving, relaxing with music or reading and taking long walks with her dog.

The Hope Master

Scott Fardulis was born in Escondido, California, a little town just east of San Diego. His father was a teacher and his mother a nurse. Scott's parents moved to La Croix, Illinois, when he was in Kindergarten. Although a suburb of Chicago, it was farmland. Scott enjoyed a Huck Finn existence playing in the wheat fields and stalking "wild animals" (mostly birds, frogs and "other interesting creatures") with his pellet gun.

Scott's parents split when he was 12 and he and his mom moved to Boulder, Colorado, to live with his uncle. As Scott says, "while we got our feet under us."

Scott spent his sophomore through senior year at a private boarding school just north of Boulder. His education was his own decision, but it was "on the pricy side," so Scott worked at the Kitty Box Factory for $3.15 an hour to pay his way. If you've seen the Discovery channel's *Dirty Jobs* series, you'll have a sense of what that was like. To this day, Scott is *not* fond of cats!

Sports kept Scott out of trouble in school.

"I loved sports," Scott said. He had natural talent and athleticism. His father was a tremendous athlete. "I used to marvel watching him play," Scott said. "He moved like a greyhound. He was fast and everybody respected him. I wanted to be as good as he was. I had a drive to go out and prove myself and push my body to the limit."

Scott became a Resident Hall Dean during his junior year in high school. He learned that he enjoyed working with people, problem-solving, and helping them through challenges.

"When you are a Hall Dean you do a tremendous amount of listening and counseling," Scott said. "I loved that. That's probably where my love for people and people skills started to flourish."

Scott's first real significant career move came in his junior year.

"One of my classmates, Cory, and I and decided that we wanted to create our own business," Scott said. "We started a window cleaning company. We got some flyers together and as soon as school got out we went door-to-door and let people know our education was important to us and we were hard workers and we were raising money to afford our school bill."

Little did the boys know what that simple, sincere "sales pitch" would turn into. That summer catapulted Scott into the entrepreneurial world far exceeding his wildest expectations. It was thrilling!

"We kept ourselves so busy," Scott said. "I don't know if it was good looks, charm, the smiles we had on our faces, the ambition that we exuded when we knocked on people's doors. We just simply asked them if we could give them free estimates to clean their windows, and with that little pitch very few people turned us down."

On a really bad day, they'd each make a couple of hundred bucks. On a good day... better. Much better. Scott bought his first car in cash and they kept their business riding for quite a while. But they came to a crossroad where they had to make a decision.

"We were both going to college," Scott said. "I wanted to go to flight school. Cory wanted to follow his dad's footsteps and be a dentist. And we were going to go away to different states. Our question was, 'How do we maintain this lifestyle?'"

"As good as we'd had it, we realized that we were trading time for money and we knew there had to be a better way."

They decided to go talk to Cory's father.

"Cory came from a family that really opened my eyes to what life could look like when it was ideal," Scott said. "Cory's parents had an incredible marriage. They were loving with each other. It was just a beautiful thing to see. Coming from a household where I watched my parents split up, I wanted that."

"They had three kids including Cory. They were honest with each other, talked about tough things, supported one another and had each other's backs," Scott said. "They travelled together. They lived in a beautiful home on acreage. They had pastures all around their house. They went to church together. Cory's dad was a big success. And I thought, this is all just so beautiful."

One day Scott asked Cory, "If we went to your dad and we asked what he would do if he was in our shoes, what do you think he'd say?" Cory said, "Let's do it." So they went and asked for his advice.

Cory's father said, "I'm glad you asked." And Scott was introduced to the world of Network Marketing. He was 17 years old.

Cory's father explained that all of his success didn't come from being a dentist. He said that in reality the lifestyle that people saw was provided by something very, very different and almost unseen.

"He invited us to a meeting that night at a hotel out East of Denver in a town called Aurora," Scott explained. "I sat in the room that night and watched him along with some others show me something that at first sat me back in my seat— and then leaned me forward on the edge of my chair. I was jaw-dropped!"

"I was being taught a concept called 'leverage,' which is what happens when you learn to use the talents of many other people to get paid as if you were working 100 or 200, or even a thousand hours yourself," Scott said. "It was polar opposite of trading time for money."

Right then and there Scott made a commitment that he was going to become a Network Marketer. He was going to work to the best of his ability, and he'd never quit. "And 25 years later," Scott said, "here we are. Sometimes people questioned me and sometimes people laughed and thought we were silly. They don't laugh anymore."

Scott's Network Marketing career has had its ups and downs, but mostly ups! That was until, at age 39, Scott experienced a health crisis that had him, literally, flat on his back.

"I couldn't walk. I couldn't move anything. I didn't want to get up to go to the bathroom, because I couldn't! I didn't even want to eat. I was depressed, discouraged, and my pain was an 11 on a scale of 1 to 10," he said. Being a glass-half-full guy all his life, Scott was beyond frustrated. He was devastated.

"For the first time in my life I didn't feel great," Scott said. "I thought, 'Okay, this is a lesson for me in learning how to relate to other people that don't feel good.' If you knew my personality you'd know that I was grasping at anything and everything. I became scared and desperate. It was hopeless. I was hopeless. It was a very tough time."

"I was betting I'd fix it myself, but I couldn't. Finally, I turned it over to God and prayed for a miracle."

That's when, out of the blue, Scott got a call from a man he hardly knew, who said, "Scott, I've heard you're going through some challenges. I'd like to meet you. I'll drive three hours to get to where you are." This was not someone Scott would have imagined would or could help. But Scott went to meet him anyway— loaded up on enough OxyContin to be able to walk and talk.

"We'd been sitting together for only a few minutes when my friend said, 'Do you know the man walking through the door right now? You need to meet him.' It was bizarre. I thought, are you serious? Meet a complete stranger? These meds are going to wear off soon. Hurry, let's get to the point. Please!"

"My friend brought this man over. You could tell they hadn't seen each other in some time. And this big guy looked right at me and said, 'You look terrible.' That was Tom Chenault, and what happened that day in that coffee shop changed my life— starting with *saved my life!*"

"That 'Coffee Shop Conversation,' as Tom calls it, lead to a chain of events that were just miracle, after miracle after miracle," Scott said. "Tom immediately got me in touch with Dr. Joel Wallach. Doc told me I could keep doing what I was doing and I wouldn't be here in 30 days— or I could do what he advised. The tears just started flowing. I was elated to hear there was hope. I did what Doc told me. And in a matter of days I was already feeling better. In just weeks I was completely well again— even better than ever before."

Scott was soon well enough to climb in a plane with Tom and fly out to California and meet the Wallach's, tour the company headquarters and learn all about Youngevity. He was in.

"Today, I've learned that nothing is more important than engaging in people's lives," Scott said. "That's what Tom did with me."

"I'll give you an example," Scott said. "How many times have you heard— or said, 'Hey, how are you?' Most people answer like I used to, 'Fine. Great. Okay,' But what if I say, 'I've been thinking about you. How are you— REALLY, *how are you?*' If I take the time... Let you know that you are on my mind... And I let you know that and I'm REALLY interested and I care about you, it's a whole different thing."

"Be real and go deep with people," Scott said, "and they will reveal to you everything you need to know to serve them. And that's what this business is really all about."

"That's probably the best tip I can give anybody about building a bigger more profitable Networking business," Scott said, "Become a master listener, asking the right questions, so you can learn how you can help. That's the agenda. Period."

"I'm a Hope Master," Scott said.

"The reward for having helped so many people achieve their hopes and dreams in life is extraordinary. It's like Zig Ziglar said, 'if you help people get what they want, all the wishes, dreams and desires of your heart become true for you and your family.'"

"That's my job: Serving as many people as possible and helping them any way I can to get where they want to go. And Network Marketing is the best way to get there I know."

"Just yesterday my son Blake, who's about to enter high school was asked to try out for the team," Scott said. "It was two in the afternoon, but I pulled him out of school early— because I could—

and we drove 30 minutes to the try-out. That time together was invaluable for my son, and for me. I got to help him prepare mentally. And I was in the bleachers watching him every minute. Every time he looked up he saw me, completely focused on him. I'm not sure any other fathers were there."

"Then, last night, my daughter had gymnastics practice. I was there. She even asked me to spot for her. I was the first person ever to see her do a back hand-spring."

"Things like that are priceless," Scott said. "You can never get time back."

"That's what freedom is: To go and do as you please with the people you care about, on a moment's notice."

"That's the freedom Network Marketing gives you."

Scott is married to Juliette Fardulis and they have three children: Blake 14, Ashton 11 and Senna who's 9. They live in the town of Loveland, in the heart of Northern Colorado.

I Got My Life Back

Dr. Corey Gold is a California boy and he's been one from day one.

"I grew up in Orange County, back in the '60s, '70s and '80s and lived in what was the quintessential Southern California bedroom community."

"My father was a schoolteacher and a vice principal. My mother was a stay-at-home mom. But my dad was pretty entrepreneurial— like a lot of teachers are— just to earn extra money. One of the things that he dabbled in was Network Marketing."

"We were the only house in the community that had a swimming pool," Corey said, "and my dad got that through Network Marketing."

Corey's father said he put the pool in the backyard, so that all the neighborhood kids would come to their house to play. "That way he could keep an eye on us. We'd always be in the backyard swimming," Corey said.

"When you're a little kid, you just see your dad go off to work. You don't know what he's doing or what your mom's doing. But my parents were using Network Marketing to help us have a better life."

"Later on, I benefitted even more from my dad's Network Marketing," Corey said, "because he had the resources to help me go to college and allow me to go get a doctorate. That was a blessing that I didn't recognize until I got older."

"Some of my best friends today are people who are legendary in Network Marketing," Corey said. "They were just pals of my parents and they lived in the same community. I was introduced to the business without really knowing it. I was just a kid and it's something my dad did."

"I had an ideal upbringing," Corey said. "Don't have a thing bad to say about it. Went to a great high school. Went to great colleges. I had and still have to this day a wonderful relationship with my parents."

"My dad's favorite thing is that he taught me to go into Network Marketing."

"He loves coming to conventions," Corey said. "He thinks it's the most fun, exciting place to be even to this day— and he's in his 80s now! He loves the energy and excitement, the entrepreneurial spirit of Network Marketing. So I make sure he's 'my date' at all our conventions."

"My mother actually started it," Corey said. "She began losing weight on the Cambridge diet and next thing she's referring all these people to get on it, but she's not getting paid. She didn't know it was Network Marketing. Eventually, somebody said to her, 'Why don't you just join the company. You're already sending people to buy products. Sign up. You can make a little extra money that way.'"

"And my mom said, 'Okay, sounds like a plan,' and next thing you know she's in Network Marketing just because she'd lost weight, people noticed, and asked her how. My parents didn't get rich in Network Marketing, but it sure made life lots more comfortable for all of us"

With such a positive exposure to

Network Marketing, why didn't Corey make that his first career choice?

"I became a Jewish dentist instead, because my Jewish parents *didn't want me* to be a dentist," Corey said. "I know. It's crazy. But you know how contrary kids can be — and that was me."

"My uncle was a dentist. I looked at him and thought, 'Hey, everyone calls this guy *doctor*. He doesn't seem to work so many hours. He has beautiful women working in his office and he takes lots of vacation time. *This is the profession for me!*' So I went into dentistry simply because I was modeling what my uncle did and what my dad didn't want me to do."

But when Corey really got into dentistry — even after eight years of school and all of that tuition money *plus* all he invested to start his practice— he began thinking, "Wow, this is not nearly as much fun as I thought it would be. I *was* a proficient dentist. I built one of the biggest practices in California, but I didn't like it. I did good work, but I didn't enjoy what I was doing. It was a groundhog day; over, and over, and over, *and* over again."

Corey admitted his profession paid the bills for his home— handsomely, too. It would put his kids through college, but it didn't feed his mind, heart and soul in any way at all. He couldn't stop thinking that there had to be a better way to live his life than come to a dental office every day. "That's what kind of got back in my head," Corey said, "and it started me thinking about what might be next."

"You know," Corey said, "my dad never thought being a dentist fit my personality. He was right. He knew me better than I knew myself."

"You have a career. You have a wife, a home. You want to have children," Corey said. "But you start thinking to yourself 'I'm stuck in this world I've created and it's not the world I want.' But you just can't quit. I was trapped."

But everything else Corey looked at meant he'd have to stop dentistry 100 percent: going back to school; opening a store of some sort. "That was a lot of risk," Corey said. "So, I was forced to consider Network Marketing, even though I rejected it repeatedly.

"I went to meeting after meeting," Corey said, "and walked out of every one thinking those people were crazy. Network Marketing was for people who couldn't do anything else. It was for people who had no education, no real profession. I'm a *dentist*, and dentists don't do these things. I was so arrogant!"

"One night, in the middle of the night, I sat up wide awake, woke my wife and said, 'Sweetheart, we are going to be millionaires!' She yawned and said 'That's great, how?' And I said, 'Network Marketing'... and *she hit me*. People laugh when I say this, but they know my wife and know it's true. She told me to go back to bed, that's silly, you're a dentist, you don't do that."

"I said, 'No, no, no. If I believe in the products, if I believe doing this will change my life, I can tell people about that company. I can do that!'"

"Like a lot of people, I was dissatisfied." Corey said. "And like a lot of people I didn't know what I wanted to do. I kept flirting with Network Marketing, because although I saw it as a powerful vehicle, my ego rejected it. Once I embraced the idea and said, 'Hey wait a second, you can make a profession of this. You can do this in a significant way. You just need to find products that you believe in.' Once I found that company — I was all in."

"I didn't know what I didn't know when I started," Corey said. "Like most people entering Network Marketing we don't know a binary from a unilevel from a stair-step. We don't know any of that stuff. We just say, 'Wow, they pay money for you to do this.'"

"So when I got in my first company, I just sat down and the person in front of me was making a great deal of money and he said, 'If you do these things the way we show you how to do them this is the kind of money you might be able to earn.' And I said, 'Sign me up.'"

"I started the very, very best way possible," Corey said. "Before I got my starter kit... Before I even got my very first order of products... I was already attending a national convention. It was perfect. I hadn't even tried the product yet and I'm sitting in a room full of 10,000 screaming believers. And thank God I was there, because I learned so much that first weekend. If I had not gone to that event, I probably would have failed."

"Because I went to that convention, Corey said, "I made connections. I understood the system. I realized that there were better ways to do the business than my instincts told me. And I saw that if I followed the plan and listened to people who were doing it well... all I had to do was follow the breadcrumbs then I'd get to the ginger bread house. And it worked."

Corey was succeeding. He was making a good check and he was one of the company's rising stars, but...

"Everything was going great," Corey said, "when my father told me, 'Corey this is a very large established company and two of our friends are starting a brand new company. We think it would be good for you to join them. They remember you as a kid. They'll watch out for you and take care of you.' So on the advice of my dad — I'd quit being a rebellious teenager — I changed companies.

That turned out, down the road 20 years, to be a wonderful decision, because it led me to where I am today."

Where Corey is today is at the top of Youngevity.

"When I first met Steve Wallach (Youngevity CEO and co-founder), one of the things I admired most about him was he had a deep, close, loving relationship to his father. He was so proud of his father. He was so loyal to him."

"I immediately knew that Steve was a man of his word. He's always been straight with me. I've walked out of every meeting with Steve and said, 'You know something, that is one of the nicest, most honest, incredible guys I've ever met.'"

"That was important to me," Corey said. "I needed a safe harbor and that's what Youngevity provided."

"I was taught by my very first leader," Corey said, "that until I was making $50,000 a month in Networking not to have an independent thought. Just follow the system. And when you're making $50,000 a month, you don't want any independent thoughts, because you understand that the system works perfectly. So I believe in using the system that Youngevity teaches us, *because* it works."

"Don't ever get too smart. Don't ever buy your own hype," Corey said. "Have a good time, learn how to laugh when you make mistakes and put heart and love into people even though you've had your heart broken before. The number one thing is that you have to get excited. When you have that energy and excitement about where you are going people just naturally want to follow you."

"It's easier to build a business fast than slow," Corey said, "because people are attracted to your success and energy. If you really want to have big success you've got to get into big action. I would tell anybody who wants to be really successful in Network Marketing that they're going to have to put their head down for a whole year or two and run like heck."

Will it be worth it?

"I've had the opportunity to see basically every one of my daughters' tennis matches," Corey said. "I've gotten to go to every single violin concert they did — even the really bad ones when they were little (they were horrible), but I got to go to all of them. I planned my day around the things that were most important to me, my wife and my kids."

"I have friends who are the same age as me; lawyers and doctors and all the great things in the world, yet they are disconnected from their families. They're going to leave a nice inheritance to their children, but I've had a chance to make a great living *and* a life with my kids that's unbelievable."

"Network Marketing is the best thing that's ever happened to me."

Corey said, "If somebody had told me you'll make just the same amount of money you do as a doctor... You'll never make one dollar more... But you'll have a much better life. I would have taken that deal alone hands down."

"I was looking for my life and I got my life back through Network Marketing."

Dr. Corey Gold and his wife Adrienne live in San Clemente, California. They put their two daughters, Sara 20 (who just graduated) and Rebecca 18 (a sophomore), through college just as Corey's dad did with him. Thanks to Network Marketing.

True Network Marketing

Blake Graham was born and grew up in Salt Lake City, Utah, and lived in the same house until he went to college. He has three brothers— one older and two younger. Blake's father was a letter carrier with the U.S. Post Office and his mother used to work at the Federal Reserve Bank, but left her job to stay at home with the kids as they grew up.

Blake did well with his classes in school. He just wasn't the most social person. He remembers going to school dances and spending the entire night without ever having the courage to ask any of the girls to dance.

"When I was at school," Blake said, "I would look at other people that were able to have conversations, the people that were able to make people laugh, and I thought that was an incredible skill. It was a skill that I didn't possess. Not that I didn't appreciate it, I just didn't have it."

"I hadn't grasped any of the principles of how to deal with people. I was growing up in a family that was all boys," Blake said. "I didn't know how to talk to girls and that was definitely reflected in my social life. But one thing I did do well, and that was to study and learn."

Blake's academic success in high school helped him earn a number of scholarships to college.

"I grew up in a Christian home where we went to church every Sunday," Blake said. "My mother was very active in the church, and going to church and having that influence I remember thinking that in the course of providing for my family I always wanted to do something that would really help people."

In college, Blake had interests in medicine, business, and in education. He started in Pre-Med, as an Economics major with a Chemistry minor.

"I interrupted college and spent a couple of years on a mission in Japan," Blake said. "Back at school in the Pre-Med program, I was asked to translate for this gentleman who was taking his Network Marketing Company over to Japan. That's really what started my career in this industry."

In the course of his translation work, Blake had been learning a lot about health and nutrition. He went to the company's meetings and heard about things like *antioxidants.* He went to his professors and asked if they really could help prevent cancer.

"My professor said it's just a bunch of lies," Blake said. "He was an MD, but in these meetings they kept quoting medical journals. I was thinking that if this company was lying, it should be pretty easy to find out. Based on my interaction with these people they seemed like good and honest folks. They didn't appear to be deceptive. In one of my college courses we learned to read medical journals, so I went and looked up antioxidants."

Through the university, Blake searched Medline®, part of the National Library of Medicine, which is part of the NIH (National Institute of Health) database of the U.S. Government.

"I was blown away to find over 800 articles going back over 20 years! This was back in the very early 1990's," Blake said. "Before nutrition really hit the world stage."

At the same time that "Pre-Med Blake" was drilling down into medical journals to learn what the MDs didn't seem to know about nutrition, "Economics Major Blake" was digging deeper into Network Marketing. While he was doing research for a major thesis on Network Marketing's unique business model, he fell in love with its concepts of residual income, the direct-to-consumer distribution channel, and the promotional and educational power of word-of-mouth marketing.

When he learned that Utah-based NuSkin International was opening up in Japan, Blake made the decision to go to Asia and join that effort.

"One of the overriding reasons was the cost of going to medical school," Blake said. "My grades were strong enough that my professors thought I could get into Harvard. But it doesn't matter how good your grades are, there are no scholarships there. You have to pay your way through. My father was a letter carrier and we lived in the lower middle-class. I was going to have to earn my way through Harvard."

So Blake went back to Japan, stood in line with 17,000 others on opening day to join NuSkin, and proceeded to struggle for three years. "I thought it would be a lot easier than it was," he said. Even though he'd built an organization of 800 people, Blake had seen many others do much better in Network Marketing than he did. It was a lot more difficult than he had envisioned.

After coming back from Japan and getting back into college, something happened that would change Blake's life: "I got a tape in the mail of Dr. Wallach's *Dead Doctors Don't Lie*, but I didn't listen to it." Blake said. "Then I got another one. I didn't listen to that either. But when I got a third tape, something struck me: Three audios, all the same, from three different people... You know the joke about the man trapped in the flood who refuses to be rescued by a Jeep, a boat and a helicopter, saying 'No thanks, God will save me?'"

"I'm in school, in Pre-Med," Blake said. "I'm in love with Network Marketing, except I don't have much to show for it. As I listened to that audio cassette it was like the scales fell off from my eyes — and I didn't even know it was Network Marketing. What impressed me most was Dr. Wallach was a veterinarian giving."

Blake knew from his four years with NuSkin, where he'd gone through all of the training on their products and talked with a lot of their top doctors and scientists, that a number of things that made that company unique were from veterinary science.

"I knew about the vital role of minerals and trace minerals that came out of veterinarian research from the U. S. Department of Agriculture," Blake said. "Veterinary medicine is decades or even centuries ahead of human nutritional research."

"So here was Dr. Wallach, not just any doctor, but a published, world-renown veterinarian and scientist. The more I heard the more I fell in love with his message."

Just a few months later, Blake ran into an old friend, Todd Smith, at a meeting (for a different Network Marketing company) a friend of Blake's was hosting. "Todd and I were freshman college roommates, back before I went to Japan," Blake said. "I had a lot of respect for Todd and that night I learned he was working with Dr. Wallach."

"I said *the* Dr. Wallach? And he was like, 'Yeah, have you heard of him?' I said, 'THE *Dead Doctors Don't Lie*, Dr. Joel Wallach?' And he said, 'Yeah.' When Todd told me Dr. Wallach was starting his own company, I started asking questions— lots of questions."

One thing Blake learned was that there were actually forty other Networking companies that were using *Dead Doctor's Don't Lie* to introduce people to their products. In total, there were more than 40 million of those tapes in circulation. When Todd told him there were only 10,000 people in Dr. Wallach's new company, the economics major, Blake did the math. "That meant there were 39 million-plus people that didn't know Dr. Wallach had his own company. This would be an amazing opportunity if the products were Dr. Wallach's proprietary formulas," he reasoned, "and if they were priced right..." They were. Blake was in.

Blake formed a partnership with Todd and the two immersed themselves in mastering the Network Marketing business model; or so they thought. Their process was as thorough and methodical as a pair of very, very bright students in Pre-Med and Law could be. They made every mistake possible. Then, they even added a few more.

"I had borrowed all the money I could from my family," Blake said, "and Todd had done the same. We had racked up quite a bit of debt trying to advertise to people and doing public health lectures. With minimum payments on credit cards, the rent, payroll— we actually had an office and a few employees— the overhead before Todd and I took a penny out of the business was $2,000 *more* than our monthly commission check!"

It didn't take an Economics major to see where their business was headed.

"That's when we had what some people call a 'Come to Jesus Meeting'," Blake said. "Do we close the doors, cut our overhead, lay off all of our staff, and spend several years paying off the $100,000 of debt we had generated, or... What? What do we do?"

That's when Todd and Blake went back to the drawing board.

Blake said, "Okay, what if—and this was a very radical concept for us—instead of advertising and trying to do it like retail sales, what if we actually do Network Marketing?"

So, they cut back advertising in newspapers and radio, had to cancel plans for a big health lecture, slashed their expenses and went out and spoke with people.

"Within less than a year," Blake said, "not only had we paid off the debt, but after all the bills were paid, there was money left over. Todd and I split the difference and I took home a $23,000 check."

"That was more money than I had made in all three previous years— and that was just one month!"

"One of the things we worked on really hard," Blake said, "was what we could do to make the business easier to understand, to make it simpler; to make it so that people can focus on keeping the main thing the main thing. We tend to over-complicate things and that slows them down."

"We did a recording called *What's Up Doc?* where I asked Dr. Wallach about specific products, why and how to use them," Blake said. "So when people heard *Dead Doctors Don't Lie* and were interested, then you'd share the next CD. It was a simple one-two process. And that's what really started to turn it around for us."

Blake compares building a multi-million dollar Network Marketing organization to the franchise business. But instead of being a single franchisee, you're the franchise company itself—like the McDonalds Corporation, you can have hundreds and thousands of successful franchisees in your Network.

"And the only way you can get 1,000 franchisees," Blake said, "is that you have to have maybe 5 or 10 that each help another 5 or 10, that help another 5 or 10 each. And just like franchising, you've got to have a proven business model people can plug into— a replicable system, and that comes back to using the very same tools and training that keep it simple and easy for people to do over and over."

"We lead with the crusade of making a difference in people's lives," Blake said.

"If you want a fulfilled life, you get it most often if you take the focus off you and put the focus on someone else."

"Someone once said, if you ever think you are overburdened with your own trouble, find somebody else with troubles and help them with theirs. As you do, your troubles are lifted."

That's what true Network Marketing is designed for," Blake said. "I can make the difference in the lives of others on a big scale by putting a system in place that helps people, help people, and then they help the next people, and they help the next people, and then they can help the next."

"There are so many people out there that need that difference. And we need more people that are making that difference in the lives of others. That's our crusade. That's true Network Marketing."

Blake Graham and his wife Naibi have three children: Emmaline, age 5; Kanai who is 2; and Bryson, who is 9 months old. They live just outside of Tokyo, Japan, and have a home in Orem, Utah, as well.

Everything Is Awesome

Dan and Mylisa Graham were both born and raised in Salt Lake City, Utah and both came from "middle-class" backgrounds.

"I was the youngest of four children," Mylisa said. "I have one older sister and two older brothers. I was the baby. The big brothers and big sister made fun of me endlessly. So, I came from an upbringing of teasing and sarcasm and I'm naturally good at those things, because I was so well trained. And, I do love them all dearly."

"I've got two younger sisters," Dan said. "The Grahams were happy and everything was going good until... The parents got divorced. It kind of was hard on us."

"At the time," Dan said, "I thought it was my fault. I couldn't understand: Why are they doing this? Years later I came to find out it was mostly over finances and their jobs. The stress was just too much for them."

"My parents were both very much blue collar workers," Mylisa said. "My dad worked for the local gas utility."

> **Mylisa's parents had a very strong belief that you started with a company, and you stayed there. You retired from that company.**

"They thought one of the most important things you could do in life was find a job with a good company that had health insurance," Mylisa said. "So that was the mentality that I had growing up."

As for school, "I was never a great student," Mylisa said, "but I wasn't a bad student. I just kind of got by."

"I think that's probably my upbringing in a nutshell," she said. "I just did everything to get by. I didn't excel at anything, but I never had a hard time with anything either. I did go to the community college for a few years. Then I took the route that my parents taught me and got a job— ironically at the same marketing company where Dan worked."

Dan had finished high school, gone on to college and was pursuing a business degree. But college just wasn't for him.

"I've always been entrepreneurial. Always been trying to do the right thing and make an extra buck," Dan said. "So out of high school, during college, I was doing landscaping; Mowing lawns, did a Christmas tree lot, that kind of stuff."

Then Dan took an abrupt detour from his business interests and became a river guide in Jackson Hole, Wyoming. He did that for a number of years, "Just trying to find out who I really was," he said. "People would tell me, 'Dan, get a life. Go get a real job.' Being a river guide, you're not making great money. You're not investing for your future. You're not doing what you need to do."

Eventually, Dan came back to Salt Lake and became a marketing rep for a company working with stockbrokers and insurance agents. He specialized in client retention and taught them how to increase their overall business and profits. And, that's where he met Mylisa. "We were really good friends at that company," she said. "We weren't dating or hadn't started dating, we were just good buddies."

It was while working at that company that a friend of Dan's approached him about an opportunity. Ever alert to anything "business," Dan was curious and open, but his friend's presentation, sketchily scribbled on a paper napkin, didn't do much for him. There just wasn't enough information to get his mind around.

"I asked about the products, and my friend said, 'Well, we don't have any products yet.' And I asked about the compensation, how I'd get paid, and he said, 'We don't have a comp plan yet.'

Then he asked me, 'Do you want to get in?' I'm like, 'No! I don't want anything to do with this!"

His friend came back to him three days later and said, "I don't understand why you're not jumping in. You need to do this." And Dan just said, "Buddy, I'm busy I don't have time." But the truth was Dan was busy being broke. He was working at the marketing firm with a nice view of the golf course, but he was broke.

"I'm sitting at my desk, in my cubicle, working extra hours trying to get promoted up to the next level, and *for the third time* my buddy is saying, 'Hey, I want you to come take a look.' So I went down and talked with him and his partner."

Then Dan did a crazy thing. "I came upstairs after meeting them and I put in my two week notice. I said, 'Okay, if we're going to do this thing we are really going to do it. We're going to do it strong and we're going to really build this business.'"

No product. No compensation plan. No idea of what he was doing. Crazy is right!

"It was the vision they painted," Dan said. "Okay, maybe it was because I had a hard day at work. Maybe the timing was right. I was 26 at the time. Maybe I was just too young. But once I figured out that I've got to do something more in order to build some kind of financial future for myself and my future family, I knew I had to make a change."

"Even though we didn't have a product at the time. Even though we really didn't really have a full compensation plan, we had a message."

What message? Dead Doctors Don't Lie.

And by the way, the buddy and his partner who got Dan involved were two of Youngevity's very first distributors: Todd Smith and Blake— no relation— Graham.

"I was probably one of the first people Dan told that he quit his job and he was going to go do this Networking Marketing thing," Mylisa said. "I thought, man he's crazy."

Mylisa had moved to Atlanta, Georgia a few years later. She and Dan had kept in touch. Mylisa let him know she was moving back to Utah. So Dan— who was doing so well in his Youngevity business and had the money and the time freedom— bought a plane ticket and flew out to Georgia to drive back with her to Salt Lake. You can learn a lot about each other on a 1,910 mile 28 hour drive; and they did.

"When we came back," Mylisa said, "Dan got me on Youngevity right away. I loved the products, but I just couldn't see me becoming involved in the business— ever. That was Dan's job. And even after we got married I was still working as an event coordinator and Network Marketing was Dan's thing."

"And it was kind of funny," Mylisa said. "I was pregnant with Zac, and Dan would do home meetings and I would leave. It was like, 'Hey, will you be done by 10?' I would call him to make sure everybody was gone, so that I could safely come home and not see anyone."

"So I'm pregnant. I'm getting up at 6:30 so I can leave the house at 7:00 to get to work. And Dan would either still be asleep or he'd be doing a conference call in his pajamas."

"Then around lunch time, I'd call him and I'd be like, 'Oh man, my boss is such a jerk today. I am so frustrated.' And he would be like, 'Oh, hun, can I call you back? I'm out on the golf course.'"

"Keep in mind that at this point, his income from Youngevity has purchased us a new home, we were both driving new cars and the money I'm making from my job, that I don't even like, is just funny money. It's not even enough to calculate into our family budget, because Dan's is paying for everything."

It was about this time that Mylisa says she finally "Got a clue" that maybe there was something in this Youngevity she needed to pay attention to.

"I'm getting ready to have this baby that I dreamed about for my whole life, and I was going to have to leave him and go to daycare," Mylisa said. "I knew I didn't want to do that. But I had enough of an independent spirit that I wanted to earn my own income. I liked to feel like I was giving back to the family."

"After a few weeks off for maternity leave with Zac, Mylisa decided she

wasn't going back to her job.

"So Dan and I sat down and I talked to him for the first time about doing Youngevity as a business. I had to look at it from my own personal standpoint, 'Okay, is this company real? Do the products work? Can I make any money?' Of course I already knew all the answers, but Dan patiently confirmed each one."

Mylisa had her struggles, just as Dan did before her. They can both tell you stories, but now they look back and laugh about them all.

"Our children have been watching the Lego movie for the last few days," Mylisa said. "One of the themes is, 'Everything *is awesome when you're part of a team.*' I think the biggest key to being successful is to be part of a team. Make yourself a team and work together. That's what Dan and I have done."

"Youngevity is a family," Dan said. "You go to one of the events, or you go and meet the staff and the corporate people, it's one team one dream. It's a family. It's a team you just want to be part of."

"What's best for me about the Youngevity business," Mylisa said, "is knowing I'm making a difference. I know Youngevity is a very unique opportunity. People will order the products not because they are Network Marketing, and not just because they need to make an income with them. They order the products because they make a difference."

"With our over 900 products, I know without a doubt that I can talk to my friends. I can talk to my family. I can talk to whomever and know and by suggesting a Youngevity product they are going to get the very best quality out there."

"And I know that by joining Youngevity," Mylisa said, "whether their goal is to make an extra $300 or an extra $30,000 a month, that's something they'll be able to do."

Dan and Mylisa Graham

"The best thing for me is I know I'm making a difference in people's lives."

"We have that residual income," Dan said. "That soft cushion that allows us to do what we want when we want. We have the time freedom. We have our health. Those three things— time, money and health— are what people want most. And with Youngevity they can have all three."

Everything is awesome indeed.

Dan and Mylisa Graham live in Sandy, Utah, a suburb of Salt Lake, where they enjoy an active 365 day outdoor lifestyle with their two boys, Zac who's 12 and Josh who's 7years old.

The Prayer

Keith Halls was born in Metairie, Louisiana. It was the very first suburb of New Orleans, located on the south shore of Lake Pontchartrain. He lived there for the first three years of his life. Then his parents moved to Nacogdoches, claimed to be "the oldest town in Texas" where Keith remained until he was 21 years old.

Keith was one of four boys who, along with their sister, grew up in a very small rental house. "We didn't really have much of anything," Keith said. The Halls were a poor family.

Like any good East Texas boy, Keith admired cowboys, loved sports and looked forward to a future in the fields— cattle, oil, blueberries. But his young life was over-shadowed by his father's severe cancer. "That was quite hard for me," Keith said.

"One night I heard a sound that really scared me. I never heard anything like it before, and I can still remember it. I got down on my hands and knees and crawled out of our bedroom. I had to find what that that sound was, because it was so scary."

It was the sound of his mother crying.

"Between sobs, my mom was telling my father that it was so hard for her to see the looks on our faces when she put us to bed hungry," Keith said. "My dad was a wonderful man and he was of course trying to calm her down and comfort her, but he was very emotional, too."

As Keith sat hunched down outside his parent's bedroom door, he wanted to burst in and shout, "Mom, dad, we're okay!"

59

The Prayer

"I stayed on my hands and knees and crawled back to my bedroom, and for the very first time in my life," Keith said. "I prayed."

"I didn't understand prayer," Keith said, "but I believed in it — mostly because I had wonderful Sunday school teachers who did. So I got on my knees that night and I prayed: 'Dear God help my parents, and please do something so they'll know we kids are okay.'"

"If you do that," Keith continued, "I'll give you everything I ever earn." But then he had the thought, 'If I do that I'll be broke, too, like my parents.' So instead he said, "I'll give you *half of everything I will ever earn in my life* — and I will help make sure that other boys and girls don't ever have to hear that sound."

Keith was convinced that he was the first seven-year old ever to over-hear his parents crying about money and not being able to feed their family.

And he did as so many people have done: Made a promise to God, but once they did, they forget all about it.

"So, as a seven year old boy, that's what I did," Keith said. "I forgot all about the promise I'd made..." [fast forward nearly 20 years] "*Until* November 23rd, 1996." Keith knows the date exactly, because that was the day that NuSkin International, the Network Marketing Company he served as Senior Executive Financial Officer, went public on the New York Stock Exchange.

"I was staying in a very wonderful hotel in Manhattan," Keith said. "It was about 7:00AM. Myself, my wife and my kids were on our way downstairs to get into a limo that would take us to Wall Street. While I was coming down in the elevator, out of nowhere, I heard a seven-year old boy's voice saying a prayer: 'Dear God, please help my parents...' and I remembered that I had promised I would give up half of everything I ever earned if God would help my parents."

"No, no, no!" Keith shouted in his head. "Not today. That's not fair. No!" Keith was all set to became a multi-millionaire, but throughout the entire day, all Keith kept hearing was that seven-year old boy's prayer over and over and over.

"That night in the hotel room I told my wife the story," Keith said. "She and I sat down and figured out exactly how much money I had earned in my career. Then, we wrote out the check. Keith has been writing checks ever since, because he made those two promises."

"And that's the reason I got involved building an organization in Network Marketing," Keith said.

"Because I believe beyond a shadow of a doubt, I can best help another person create an income that can truly change their life in this great industry."

"That prayer fashioned my life," Keith said. "Every day that I'm out there building my business, I think of a seven year-old that won't have to hear their mother crying and be scared like I was. So I do my best to help people get an extra $550, $1500, $2,500 a month, because I promised God I would."

But if you'd asked anybody in his high school graduating class if Keith would be successful, you'd probably hear them laughing at you. Keith didn't take school as seriously as he should have. Part of that was because of his insecurity, "We never had most of the things that other kids did," Keith said.

The Prayer

Keith did have the grades, barely, to get into a university. Just before he started college, his father sat him down told him, "Keith, you may have played while you were in high school, but the next four years will determine how you spend the rest of your life. Now, you have to get serious. "

That was exactly what Keith needed to hear, and he got serious. His first degree was from Steve F. Austin University, in Political Science. He graduated *Cum Laude,* and went on to Brigham Young University for his second degree, in Accounting.

"After graduation, my wife and I lived in one of these run-down apartment complexes," Keith said. "And in that same unit were two gentleman, Blake and Brooke Roney. One night, Blake said, 'Keith, I want you to go play basketball with me,' and I did."

"Forgive me for saying this, but Utah was kind of a boring place," Keith said. "Everybody was in bed by 9:30, so we went to the local church to play basketball at 10 o'clock. After we finished playing that night Blake said, 'Keith I'd like to talk about our future,' and I said, 'What do you mean?'"

Blake told Keith that he was starting a company that would sell world class products using a system of sales and distribution called Network Marketing. That drew a blank look from Keith.

Blake asked, "Have you ever heard of it?" Keith said, "No."

Blake asked, "Have you ever heard of Amway?" Keith said, "No."

Blake exclaimed, "What! Where have you been in your life?"

Keith laughed and Blake started drawing circles on the gymnasium floor.

"As I watched him it was amazing, because more than anything I sat there thinking, 'I wish I had that much confidence in *my* future.' I mean, I'd graduated top of my class, but he was *so confident*. Plus, he started talking about leveraging and as a boy I'd started my own lawn mowing business, so I knew all about leverage."

Late one night, Blake formally asked Keith if he would be part of the company. Even though the word "No" was about to come out of his mouth, because he'd planned to go to law school, Keith said, "Yes. Yes. I'd be happy to. In fact, I'll be elated to be part of this company."

Keith was one of the founders and served as the senior financial executive of $1.5 billion-dollar NuSkin International for 17 years.

He left the company to become a Network Marketer.

"I remember every month looking at checks for individuals who hadn't worked for 10 or even 15 years," Keith said. "And I thought 'I want that, too.' I knew that if I quit NuSkin someday, as wonderful as they were, they weren't going to pay me after I stopped working. I wanted to be able to have a life-long residual income."

Keith also made a comment that one day, he would go out and put into practice what he'd been preaching and teaching. Not wanting to interfere in anyone else's business, nor have an unfair advantage, he chose to leave NuSkin and find a smaller younger company.

The Prayer

"The first nine or 10 months, I set so many records for failure I hold the mark for that," Keith said laughing. "I mean, I avoided picking up that phone for so many days I could have sworn that receiver weighed a ton. And I'd hold meetings and nobody would come. I held one catered dinner at my house and I had invited two couples to come over. And that night I blew out the candles and took the food to a homeless shelter because nobody came."

One night, on the verge of quitting, Keith had a dream about his Dad who had been shot down and trapped behind enemy lines in World War II Germany. In his dream Keith's father told him, "If I had quit you wouldn't be here today." Keith he said, "I know your future and it's bright. You can't quit." Seconds later Keith woke up and started writing what turned out to be "The Nine Rules for Success in Network Marketing," which is now a book.

1. Dream the dream

2. Believe

3. Treat your business as a business

4. Never quit

5. Work, talk and act from the heart

6. Trust

7. Ask for help

8. Be nice, be kind and help others

9. Massive action brings results

"I knew where they came from," Keith said.

"I put those Nine Rules into practice and my check literally went from a couple of hundred dollars a month to over one hundred thousand a

month in a period of a year."

Keith joined Youngevity after he completed a financial consulting project for the company. "As I got to know Steve Wallach, I knew (that) here was a man filled with total integrity. His word was his bond. And in his humble way, he would not only be able to guide Youngevity to a hundred million, I knew he was the man that could also take it to one billion and above."

"The key to success in Network Marketing," Keith said, "is just learning to think more about John Doe's check than I think about my own."

"That's the very best thing for me. Seeing other people be able to receive their checks" Keith said. "Because I still believe that if I could help people get a check of $500 or $1,500, then there's a seven year old somewhere who doesn't have to hear what I did."

"If you take a person that is struggling with life or struggling with whatever it might be, yet you are bringing them hope and then watch that hope blossom into a reality. That's the greatest thing in the world for me," Keith said.

"Two thousand years ago, a preacher from Galilee taught us, 'Whosoever shall compel thee to go one mile, go with him two.' You just have to be willing to do more for a person than they are willing to do for themselves."

Keith Halls lives with his wife Heather and two of their six children – Erica who's 13 and Mark age 8 – in Orem, Utah. Along with their other Halls' children, Christina, Rebecca and the other Mark, they have never heard their parents crying in the middle of the night.

A Life Long Fascination

_____

Paul Kroto was born, raised and still lives in Buffalo, New York. "I have two great parents that I owe my whole life to," Paul said. "We were very Christian-based with great family values. There's lots to be said about paying attention to your kids and raising them right, because it pays off in the long run for sure. I'm really so grateful for my parents."

"My mom has a ton of common sense and my dad was a guy that was super, super smart. He got all 4.0s in high school and college. My dad was a computer programmer and my mother was a nutritionist. I tell people I'm a combination of both of them."

Paul's mom always made healthy meals for the family. "There was a juicing machine in my house— nobody else I knew had one— and she would make fresh smoothies with different fruits and vegetables and things," Paul said.

His mom worked as a nutritionist at a hospital and a couple of different health organizations. She was involved with Shaklee vitamin products for a while, so Paul picked up a little Network Marketing experience at home and even attended some training meetings with her as well.

That began a life-long fascination with nutrition for Paul.

"When I went to high school, I took a nutrition class," Paul said. "I think I was the only guy ever to do that in the history of West Seneca West High School."

"I have a sister that's a couple of years younger than me," Paul said. "And we both turned out, I guess what you'd call pretty

67

good. I know our parents are very proud of us for the things we've been able to accomplish in life."

"When I was a child we played outside all the time," Paul said. "I was out from 7:00 am to dusk every single day. I loved playing — *anything*. If I had a ball or a puck I'd play with it. In high school I played soccer and football, ran track, was on the basketball team, skied. So I was heavily, heavily involved in sports. In weight-lifting too."

"I always wanted to be strong back in high school. For a young boy it's hard to gain weight and get bigger," Paul said. "So I'd be lifting weights and eating a lot of protein and trying to build muscles. I enjoyed those days when I could eat whatever I wanted."

Paul was a decent student. He got B's and A's. His parents made sure he did his homework every night. Paul's sister was just like his dad. She got straight A's in everything. Effortlessly.

"We were a middle-class family," Paul said. "We didn't have a ton of money. We weren't what you'd consider rich, but we weren't poor either. It was going to be a stretch for my parents to pay for my college. That was during Desert Storm back in '91, and I felt the calling to serve my country. So I decided to join the Marines."

Paul enlisted when he was still in high school. He finished his senior year and got his diploma. He'd turned into a pretty brilliant student, graduating with honors at the top of his class.

"The Marines was an experience. I just went in for the four years. They had an unbelievable college deal back then, where I could take classes at a very discounted rate, and they were going to give me $50,000 towards college. I sure didn't want to be one of those students that walked out of college with $100,000 in debt," Paul said.

Paul immediately fit right in with the Marines. He loved the military lifestyle; the schedule, the self-discipline. He got out in 1994 and started studying for his Master's Degree at the University of Buffalo. He also got a job at Gold's Gym, working there to make extra money. Paul was a full-time student and was also working full-time.

"That's when my whole life changed— quickly," Paul said. "When I got home, my grandmother had just received this audio tape in the mail. Out of the blue. She knew I was going for my Master's and how much I loved nutrition. She said, 'Paul, you need to hear this. I have no idea how they got my address or why they mailed this to me, but you need to listen to it. I think you're going to find it fascinating. '"

"So I got it from her and listened. From that moment on I knew what I was going to do with my life, I was going to follow and preach this message to people."

The title of that audio tape was *Dead Doctors Don't Lie.*

"I guess I was one of the first people to get it back in 1994," Paul said. "I called the number on the cassette and talked to a gentleman who told me about the company and the doctor on the tape. His name was Dr. Joel Wallach."

"I didn't 100 percent believe in what they were teaching in college," Paul said. "But it was a good basic knowledge of how the human body works and how nutrition works. What I heard on

Dead Doctors... was way above and beyond that! I became very passionate about it."

Working at Gold's, Paul was able to pass out the audio to gym members and that gave him a great jump-start for his business. "I had no idea what the letters 'MLM' even stood for," Paul said. "I just knew I had an audio tape and the guy on the phone told me to pass them out to people and I could make money. If people bought, they'd send me a check."

So that's what Paul did and he started making money. Then another life-changing experience came along.

"I was at a New Vision conference— the company I was with at the time. There was a table there with a whole bunch of tools on it; audio cassettes and CDs and videos, and all kinds of stuff. There was one video called *Brilliant Compensation*. Great title! The guy standing next to me said this is a phenomenal video. So I brought it, brought it home, but it was sitting around for about a month or two before I got around to watching it."

"One night, I had nothing better to do, saw it lying there and decided to watch it," Paul said. *"That* really changed my life, because I didn't understand the concept of Network Marketing or MLM, and once I watched it— I actually watched it three times in a row that night— I told my wife I wanted to quit work right away!"

After watching Brilliant Compensation, Paul just couldn't get himself to go back to a job.

"It just hit me so hard," Paul said. "There's just a better way of living."

Paul was doing the math. He was able to pay off a lot of his regular college, but his Master's Degree cost him $125,000. He owed money on that, and his apartment, and a car and trying to have some sort of a life. The math didn't add up.

"I just didn't have enough money coming in," Paul said. "I started thinking about my future and where I wanted to go. My dad, even though he was a computer programmer, he never worked for anybody. He was always self-employed, signing deals as people needed him and he was in very high demand. My mom was the same way— and she was involved in Shaklee. So I had an upbringing of being an entrepreneur, but I had no idea what this Network Marketing model was about until I saw *Brilliant Compensation*. I got it!"

Paul was with a team in New Vision that was taking some massive action. Paul was mailing out about 1,000 audio tapes a week and he did that for four years. Massive action indeed.

"We had it down to a system," Paul said. "We had mailing labels, the audios, the envelopes. My kitchen became a factory for mailing out audio tapes and my wife would help. We'd be up to the wee hours of the morning just putting stickers on envelopes and on audio tapes to get them out."

Paul was able to make an incredible income doing that. He quickly hit the seven-digit mark— one of 44 people that became millionaires giving out *Dead Doctors Don't Lie* tapes.

But it didn't last. The government prohibited the distribution of the tape; disputing some of the claims that were being made. Ironically, Dr. Wallach proved that the tape was actually 100% accurate— well, not completely, as he'd said the average age of the doctors was 58 and it was only 56— and he was completely vindicated in court seven times. But handing out the tapes came to a dead stop at that time, and so did Paul's business.

A Life Long Fascination

Paul joined another company and was once again blessed to catch another rocket to the moon. Being a nutritionist, Paul was very good at telling the story, but without something like *Dead Doctors Don't Lie*, Paul himself had to become the tool.

"The product was great," Paul said, "but because I believed so much in Dr. Wallach's mission, I knew it didn't provide people with the core 90 essential nutrients they needed."

Paul soon learned about a new company owned by Steve Wallach called A.C.T., Advanced Cellular Technology. Paul met Steve, and they launched the product with "absolutely phenomenal growth." Eventually, A.C.T. Merged with Youngevity. And Paul started building his Youngevity business.

Paul felt like he'd finally come home, where he belonged.

"Success in this business has everything to do with being with the right company," Paul said. "A company with the right message. A company with the right tools. A company with the right products— and all at the right time. That makes all the difference in the world. And right now, the only company that has all that is Youngevity."

"So my message to people is that there is hope for you, because there was hope for me."

"I was just a school kid from West Seneca, New York, a little suburb in Buffalo," Paul said. "I had a middle class background, yet I was able to create this amazing income and amazing lifestyle, simply by using a powerful tool with a compelling message and sharing it with people. Meeting new people every day. Really focusing on connecting with them and leading with my heart. Sharing that message— a message of health and wealth that I'm passionate about."

"I'm so very grateful to the Wallach's. Youngevity is the perfect situation. You've got to have a group of people that all have a strength. We all have our wheel house of what we are good at and it's important to focus on your strengths," Paul said.

"Steve Wallach is the greatest product guy in the (industry) — and he's a super-sharp business leader. Dr. Wallach's got the most amazing health message Network Marketing has ever heard. It is indisputable. *Dead Doctors Don't Lie* is the number one educational tool ever created."

"And then to have Bill Andreoli come in and really get out there and manage the day-to-day stuff, just getting all the boats going in the right direction. That's what allows all the other people to do their jobs. There is just a great situation going on here with Youngevity."

"Everyone is playing their role to perfection," Paul said. "And when everyone plays their position — and we have such strong players in each position — it just makes for a perfect storm. All things are clicking 100 percent.

"It makes me get up at 6:00 AM every morning," Paul said. "And I stay up till midnight and 2:00 AM."

"90 For Life is a crusade. It's something that changed my life and it's something that I will do forever."

Paul Kroto and his wife Vaso, who's an entrepreneurial restaurant owner, live in Buffalo, New York, with their two very special dogs: Kody a Samoyed Husky from Siberia, and Kalika, a Shiba Inu, descended from the ancient dogs of Japan.

The Blessings of a Lifetime

Sheryl Morley is the oldest of seven children and spent the first 8 years of her life on a chicken farm in Eagle, Idaho, where her dad worked. That is until the family was able to build a home of their own on her grandfather's land next door.

"We milked the cows in the morning," Sheryl said. "We fed the chickens and collected the eggs. We had English cattle, so we took care of them, too. We had a one-acre garden, which was wonderful— the weeding was *not* that wonderful— and I also had a paper route."

> **"That was just so much work. It was hard growing up on a farm," Sheryl said. "But the thing I've always been grateful for is that it really taught us a great work ethic."**

"And it *was* fun," Sheryl said. "I had two brothers and four sisters and my mom was out a lot of the time, so I was kind of left in charge a lot. I'm not sure my brothers and sisters liked that very much. I ran a pretty tight ship."

Sheryl had a lot of challenges and problems in school. "Now I think it's because I had ADD or ADHD," Sheryl said. "But back then we really didn't know about those things. It was just very difficult for me to comprehend and remember the things I read, and it was very hard for me to pay attention."

With those two things going against her, it was pretty difficult. She really didn't get much out of school. She spent most of her time just trying to pass whatever grade she was in. Sheryl went through school never feeling like she would amount to much.

"It really hurt my sense of self-esteem," Sheryl said. "In the home I grew up in, it was wonderful for the boys to go to college, so that they could provide for their families. But for the girls... I don't ever remember us being encouraged to continue on after high school. It was all about finding a nice guy and getting married and having a family."

"I didn't really have any dreams then," Sheryl said. "Mostly just the fear of, 'Oh my gosh! What if I can't find a nice guy?' That's what I remember most growing up: 'What if nobody likes me? What if there's nobody out there that will want to marry me?'"

Sheryl didn't suffer from low self-esteem– she simply just didn't have any.

"The dreams I had were very limited," Sheryl said. "As I grew up I just really wanted to be a cocktail waitress. I thought that that would be something great that I could do."

"And actually... "Sheryl said. "You know those girls on the road crew who stand there and hold the stop & go sign? I thought, 'I could do that. That doesn't look that hard. I don't mind standing out in the sun all day long.' My dad told me they made $10 an hour. I said, 'That right there is the job for me.'"

Sheryl did, just barely, graduate from high school, and because she had to take summer classes to do so, she never did "take the walk" at graduation. "I'll never forget the Vice Principal of my school saying, 'You know Sheryl, the problem with you is you are just too hard-headed. I really doubt that you are ever going to amount to anything.'"

Sheryl sat there thinking, "He's probably right. I'll never amount to anything." She just felt like her life was going nowhere. She had no idea how she was going to survive, and she felt really, really alone. Her dad always used to tell her, "Don't worry, Sheryl, this too shall pass." It did, but like her grades, not by much.

After graduating, Sheryl did in fact become a cocktail waitress. And at 26, she found herself doing all sorts of different jobs — anything and everything she could do to survive. And then the chance of a lifetime showed up.

"I mean, this was my dream job!" Sheryl said. "I could not believe someone was even considering me for this position... My good luck... My good fortune... And oh my gosh all of the stars were shining on me. I sent out cards. I told everybody in my world, 'I am the new Assistant Manager of Taco Bell!' I had never in my life been so excited or so pleased about anything. I just couldn't believe it. Things were finally starting to happen for me."

About two or three months into her "great, new, fantastic... job," Sheryl realized what being an assistant manager really means: Whenever somebody's sick — give Sheryl a call. Whenever somebody's tired or just doesn't come into work that day — well, that's Sheryl's job. Closing up late at night — Sheryl will do it. Opening up early in the morning — Sheryl will do it.

"I was absolutely shocked that this dream job of mine was really nothing more than working longer, harder and getting paid the exact same amount as everybody else."

Sheryl didn't feel real good about that. She'd also begun to have the effects — and the pain — of arthritis. Plus, she started gaining weight. One of the "perks" of being an assistant manager at Taco Bell was that you got to eat and drink all you wanted for free.

"So I was having fast-food, junk-food three times a day," Sheryl said. "My weight was ballooning out of control. The doctor said I did indeed have arthritis, but he told me, 'There's nothing you can do about it.' Then he told me when I got older I'd need double knee replacements and who knows what else. It really, really scared me. They gave me medication, which just made me gain more weight— and it made me really groggy. I had a hard time waking up and getting to work on time."

"I didn't know what to do," Sheryl said, "so I talked with my mom. She told me, 'You don't need those painkillers. Listen to *Dead Doctors Don't Lie* and get on this fantastic product. That will take care of your arthritis.'" Sheryl didn't believe her.

"Absolutely not!" Sheryl said. "I'm not going to listen to any 'Dead Doctors' anything!"

After three months or so, Sheryl finally did listen. It changed her life.

"I could not believe that doctors were telling me there was nothing that they could do, and this Dr. Wallach— who was a veterinarian, of all things— was saying it was just a nutritional deficiency. I could fix myself. I wouldn't be in pain. I would be able to run. I would be able to do all these things that I wanted to do." Sheryl was amazed.

Still, she couldn't believe it would really help, or that it would make a difference. But it did. It made all the difference in the world.

"I decided that if I could fix my problem," Sheryl said, "then what about all these other people I knew that were having health challenges. I didn't know anything about the business, but I did know that I believed in these products and I did want to tell people about them."

Sheryl's mom explained that she'd been working for Terry Porter, and he worked with Dr. Wallach (Doc). "Mom asked me if I'd like her to see if she could get me a job with him," Sheryl said. "It wasn't a hard decision for me to leave Taco Bell. I moved from Arizona back to Boise, Idaho, and I started working for Terry Porter."

Sheryl would speak on the telephone, share her experience with people and sell them Dr. Wallach's products. Then, Terry and Dr. Wallach started doing health seminars together.

"I helped them put together the seminars," Sheryl said. "We would do maybe three, three and a half weeks out of every month. I got to know Dr. Wallach really well, and I realized he was a man on a mission. He has a *huge* heart and was really committed to helping people."

It fascinated Sheryl that Doc was as healthy as could be. He had all the money he wanted. Had a lovely wife. Had a wonderful family. He had everything he personally needed, but instead of saying "I'm great and everything is good for me," he was on a mission to change the lives of millions of people worldwide.

Remember the once-upon-a-time aspiring road-crew/cocktail waitress who didn't know how to dream?

That was changing for Sheryl big time.

She bought into Doc's dream so completely that when the opportunity came to work for him directly, she jumped at it. Sheryl started managing all of Doc's health seminars. She handled the logistics and all the arrangements. And the girl who'd never been on an airplane before, found herself traveling all across the US, and around the world.

There came a point when Dr. Wallach and those closest to him decided that they would start their own company. Doc said, "The way we change America through health is with the products, and the way that we change America through wealth is with Network Marketing. I want to give everybody the chance to make more money and to realize their dreams."

Dr. Wallach sat Sheryl down and told her she had one of two choices: She could continue to work for the corporate office managing his seminars for a set salary, or Sheryl could have a downline— she'd be her own boss with no limit to her potential, but there were no guarantees either.

Sheryl told Doc, "Network Marketing."

Doc told Sheryl, "Good answer."

"I had the absolute blessing of a lifetime," Sheryl said. "I became the very first distributor in Youngevity."

Dr. Wallach told Sheryl it wasn't going to be easy. He said, "You'll have to work all the time— work, work, work, work, work. That's all there was to it." Sheryl didn't mind working hard. "Dr. Wallach was really a fantastic mentor for me," Sheryl said. "He taught me how to talk to people, how to follow-up and have relentless patience, and how to build an organization."

Sheryl learned and implemented the lessons Doc taught her so well that after 10 year years of hard work, she achieved a dream few in this business ever accomplish. She took eight years off to be with her husband and start a family.

"I stayed home, raised my kids, and the whole time my check from Youngevity continued to go up. It was a fantastic experience," Sheryl said. "Then, when I knew that my kids were going to start kindergarten, I had to think about what I really wanted to do. I'm not the type to sit around and do nothing (even if I am getting paid for it). I decided I was going to go back to actively work Youngevity."

"The reason I did," Sheryl said, "was because I have such a passion for the products and for the way that Dr. Wallach has set up this company. His mission is engrained in me. It's in my soul."

"Yes the products have changed my health and the way I feel," Sheryl said. ("And you can forget those double knee replacements.") "But the business opportunity and the income that I am so blessed to make have truly changed my life. "

"I just want to share that so badly with other people... people who are like I used to be. I want to give other people a chance to do what I've done."

"It's so funny," Sheryl said. "Every morning I wake up and I think. 'Okay, I know there's somebody out there who won't learn the message of hope for their health or wealth if I don't share it with them.' That's what really drives me. That's what really keeps me going. I'm on a mission— the same mission that Dr. Wallach's on— to get this message of Health and Wealth out to the world, and I love it!"

Sheryl Morley lives in Clifton, Virginia, with her husband Jonathan Emord (the attorney who partnered and pioneered Dr. Wallach's challenges to the FDA) and their two children, Justice and Angelica, both 6 years old and... both twins.

It Happened For Us

Barb and Dave Pitcock were both born and raised in Kansas. Barb started and stayed in Russell, where the Pitcock family lives today. Dave is originally from Park City, about 2 and-a-half hours "as the pickup rattles" from Russell.

Kansas is called "The Great Plains" for a reason— flat, broad and vast. And most things in Kansas, that's almost dead center of the U.S., are small. Even the big cities are pretty little compared to other metro areas across the country. Kansas, however, is covered with small, but very close-knit communities filled with even closer knit families, which form the indelible fabric of Middle America.

Barb was the oldest of five.
Dave was the oldest of two.

"My dad worked and my mum worked— some," Dave said. "But she mostly stayed home with my brother and I. We grew up at a time when your mom said, 'Get out of the house, it's nice outside. And don't come home until dark.' So I spent my life either playing baseball or kickball, or at a swimming pool, or fishing— or beating up on my brother (he was four years younger) and his friends. That was kind of my entire youth."

"I was the oldest of five and my mom stayed home with us until the third grade," Barb said. "My dad worked for a cement company and helped my grandparents with a RV park & camp ground, and a bunch of rentals. My grandpa was an entrepreneur. They owned a lot of properties and we grew up always helping them. We were real family-business oriented."

When Barb was in the third grade, her parents started a food and dairy distribution business. They began with one tractor-trailer truck and pretty soon they had two. They were workaholics, so

Barb's mother was gone almost all the time and Barb ended up raising the "babies."

"They were so busy making a living," Barb said, "there wasn't much time to make a life with us kids. They also bought a grocery store, owned a Sonic drive-in, a golf course, the camp ground and about 16 or 17 rental houses... Then my dad left."

It was prom night and Barb was a candidate for queen. That's when her dad handed her mom divorce papers. He stayed until graduation, then disappeared. Barb didn't see him again until four years later— on her wedding day.

"I didn't know where he was," Barb said. "He changed his name and my mom raised us with no husband. So my idea of going to college kind of got all wrecked."

"In the month of May, my senior year of high school, I was going to the Pueblo ballet in Pueblo, Colorado, because my dance instructor had moved out there. That's what I really wanted to do. But then... Long story short: I settled for beauty school back home, because I could commute and help my mum raise the kids."

Dave had a scholarship to play baseball in college. He thought he wanted to go to veterinary school, but he changed his major— many, *many* times.

"What I really learned in college," Dave said, "was I just didn't like college."

"I like to think my work ethic is pretty good," he said. "I'll try to outwork *any*body, but I found myself not wanting to do *any*thing in college. So, I moved around; from veterinary to criminal justice; from playing baseball to going for my professional rodeo card. I tried to ride bulls for about eight years. I was a free spirit. That may be the best way to put it."

It was a time in Dave's life when he was searching — for a goal, an adrenaline rush, something that was bigger than he was. He rode some. Made a little money here and there. Rodeo people say, "It's not if you get hurt, it's when, and how bad." That was the story with Dave's rodeo career.

"I'd been hurt a bit," Dave said. "Ended up with a couple of concussions. Then I broke my leg really bad in 1993. I had to move home and camp out on my mum's couch for a month or two. I couldn't really do anything with a leg that was completely shattered. I had to spend two weeks in the hospital before I could come home. That's actually how I met Barb. When I was lying on my mum's couch with my leg trashed."

Barb's sister was sweet on Dave's brother. One morning, she brought him breakfast and Barb came with her. There was Dave on the couch; cut off shirt, hair all down in his face (he hadn't had a haircut in who knows how long), and he didn't smell so good either. He couldn't shower or bathe with his leg messed up, so...

Barb and Dave have been together from that day – for more than 20 years now.

However, at that moment, Dave was engaged to another girl and Barb to another guy! Dave called Barb, the beautician, and asked if she made house-calls and would give him a haircut. He also told her he had two tickets to... But the truth is, he lied. He didn't have tickets to anything. He just wanted to see Barb.

"When Dave and I got together, we were instantly best friends," Barb said. "His dad left his mom. My dad left us. Our stories were so similar that when we started talking, we would just go on for hours. We spoke about all of our feelings, our mums, why did this happen, that... I mean, he was just my best friend long before we were in love. It was crazy. I think all along God had a plan. Honestly, that's why I think Dave broke his leg and ended up needing me to give him a haircut."

"The night that we really got together," Barb said, "I had come home after taking my little brothers and sisters to a rodeo, and the guy I was engaged to was really, really drunk and pretty abusive. My sister was crying, trying to break it up. I finally left and took off down the road to town."

Dave drove downtown that night in his little Pontiac Fiero with his foot propped up and his crutch sticking out the window. He had his friends drop him off at the parking lot on Main Street.

"I was sitting there in tears trying to figure out what to do," Barb said. "I got a big old hiking boot stomped in the middle of my back. I can't go home because this guy is stupid drunk. I'm just like, '*What am I going to do...?*'"

"I truly didn't feel like I had much to live for. I felt... I don't know, just so lost."

Right then Barb looked up. Dave was standing there at her window — and his friends were driving away in his car.

"I said, 'Man, you can't get in my car; I have a crazy boyfriend, he'll kill you,' and Dave just said, 'Okay, lets drive out to the country.' And I thought, 'Well that's a novel idea. We'll get killed together.' But we drove to the country and we talked until four in the morning. We plotted how we were going to run away together — and that's what we did. We ran away to Cody, Wyoming."

Barb and Dave Pitcock

"I ran away with a rodeo cowboy," Barb said. "I thought we were just going to go rob the world in Cody. We called off our weddings and left."

"Our parents were in absolute shock. My mom was actually looking for my dad to sign papers to get me committed. They thought I was having a breakdown and I needed to be put in a rubber room. I owned a dance school and I had a beauty shop, and I just ran away. "And," Barb said, "I have never been so homesick in my life."

When the runaways got to Wyoming, Dave was still all busted up. He had several knee surgeries. He couldn't get a job. Barb couldn't get a job either. The former beauty shop owner was begging just to cut hair. They had nothing. They stood in the food pantry line for beans and sardines.

"We were young," Barb said. "And we were having second thoughts. Like, *what the heck have we done here?* Dave wanted to go to the courthouse and get married right away, so we weren't living in sin. I wanted to have the big show wedding I'd always dreamed of. And you know what happened?"

Barb and Dave went back home. They got a little log cabin, brought their family and friends together and got married and started having babies. And yes, Barb's dad *did* show up for the wedding.

Dave started to work construction, but the only job he could get was far away, so he was gone Monday through Friday. "I would leave Barb and our baby Brookyn, and go on my way to dig ditches. That was our life. We just worked— and paid bills, and got in debt and wrote bad checks and bought a whole bunch of diapers, because we had another kid a year later and that was our life."

"Barb has this entrepreneurial spirit," Dave said. "When she looks at you and tells you something, she puts you in a trance and you just do what she says. So she looked at me one day and said, 'We're going to start our own business.'"

Dave's grandmother had taught him how to refinish furniture, so he opened up a little shop refinishing antiques. Barb opened a hair store and a dance studio for little girls in the same building.

"We worked hard at our businesses to try to make it big," Dave said. "But you know what? We were happy. We felt like we were kind of in control of our lives."

It was November of 1995 and Dave's best friend was talking to him one day, and gave him a video tape. He said, "Dave, you and Barb need to look at this. This company is getting ready to do some amazing things. I think they can make a ton of money. You need to check this out." Dave said, "Sure," and put the tape in the back of his pickup— where it sat for three months.

One day, Dave's friend was back. "The thing I've been telling you about," he told Dave, "there's a meeting in town tonight. We need to go." Dave went.

"It was the first time in my life I'd heard or seen somebody put a big circle up on a whiteboard and write the word *Dreams* in bold above it," Dave said. "This guy started asking: 'What would you do if you were making extra money? What would you do if you won the lottery?' And I'm sitting there and the more he talked, the more excited I got."

Barb and Dave Pitcock

"Long story short," Dave said. "I joined. It was March of 1996. I didn't know why I got in. I didn't know how it worked. I just got involved because I was ready for something — *anything* — and I was excited."

"I called Barb on my way home," Dave said. "It cost $1,035 that we didn't have, but I joined. I called Barb and she said, 'Dave, *why did you do it!?!*'"

"You didn't ask me. You didn't talk to me. We've been married five years and we have kids. We don't have a thousand dollars."

"It's Network Marketing. I've been in those before. Our closet is full of kits. They don't work. I sponsored 54 people in Amway and my biggest check in two years was $64! You're an idiot!"

"Good luck," Barb said. "But don't talk to any of my friends, and don't bring it in my salon, and don't tell our family and leave our pets out of it!'"

Dave can't remember if he slept on the couch that night or stayed out in his furniture trailer. "I'm not even sure I went in the house," he said.

"I've heard the phrase so many times," Dave said, "When you're excited the facts don't count. For the first time in my life somebody showed me how to leverage my time. I didn't know you could work four hours and get paid like you worked 40 hours. I mean that concept blew my mind."

"And residual income: You work one time and you keep getting paid and paid and paid. I remembered that video tape in my truck, so I went and got it and I played that thing over and over again

89

hoping that Barb would hear something... That she would get excited about *something.*" It didn't take very long.

"You know what?" Barb said. "This *is* interesting. They've really solved all the headaches. All the reasons that I hated Network Marketing and I'm so negative about it. Everything I'm listening to, they've changed all that. I like it."

It wasn't two weeks before Barb was more excited than Dave was. And the rest, as they both say, is history.

"It's not when you get in Youngevity," Dave said, "it's when Youngevity gets in you! That's when your life just takes off."

"I've done it good and I've done it wrong. I've struggled in my business. Had ups and downs. But when I'm on the same page with myself and I know why I'm doing this, I get out of my way. When you make it about your own goals and dreams, that transfers over to wanting to help other people do the same."

"Seeing other people's dreams come true and how you changed their lives, it's pretty emotional," Barb said. "Just to know that this business gave them their lives back."

"It's just a better way," Dave said. "I think sometimes what holds people back, and why they won't go build it, is because they don't really know what they have in their hands. We grew up our whole lives trading time for money. If I work 40 hours, I get paid 40 hours. Leverage and residual income makes you free."

"My favorite part of Network Marketing is Network Marketing."

"I can't imagine what our lives would have been like if I was still cutting hair and Dave was building furniture, trying to put kids through college and get cars and all that happens when you're raising a family," Barb said.

"Youngevity makes your outcome like a fairy tale. It's just one of those things that you never dream could happen and it just seems so farfetched. And then when it happens for you it just goes and goes and goes."

"It happened for us. We want it to happen for everybody else."

—————————————————————

Barb and Dave Pitcock have three children; Brooklyn who's 20, Chance 19 and Kali 17, who's still at home. They still live in Russell Kansas, although they're spending more and more time away, traveling the Network Marketing rodeo circuit.

We Are Making History

Ernestine Ray was born and grew up with her older sister in Brooklyn, New York, home of one the greatest "melting pots" of ethnic and cultural variety in America. That was a good thing for Ernestine, whose mother is Caribbean— from the island of Jamaica— and her father was both Native American *and* African American. Cultural diversity has been a way of life for Ernestine throughout her life.

"The values that were stressed in our home," Ernestine said, "were good education, diligence, independence, close family ties and absolutely striving for excellence."

Yet in spite of that, Ernestine struggled as a child. She was mistakenly classified as "Learning Disabled."

"My older sister was very, *very* brilliant," Ernestine said. "In fact she skipped from second to fourth, fifth, and then sixth to eighth grade, which made the fact that I was mislabeled as I was even *more* difficult for me. I was ostracized in many ways; laughed at; called names. I mean it was not pretty. Not a pleasant childhood at all."

Ernestine found herself in classes that were way beneath her abilities— and there simply were no expectations encouraging her to become better.

But there was one silver lining: She was able to move freely around the school, because she was the only child that wasn't disobedient in class. "They allowed me to go to the library and do things that other students didn't have the opportunity to do."

"That librarian was a gift from God." Ernestine said, "She was a mentor for me. If it wasn't for her, who knows where I would be today." The librarian helped Ernestine learn to read and that opened up a whole new world for her.

"I had a third grade teacher that talked about people living in trees," Ernestine said. "She was probably joking, but I was fascinated. So I asked the librarian 'where are these people that live in trees?' and they had tails, and... She started laughing and said, 'I know what you're talking about,' and she showed me some books on Africa. I was so interested in finding out more about these people because they kind of looked like me."

And Ernestine did find out more; lots more. She not only learned to read, she left that "learning disability" so far behind she graduated from high school with scholarship offers galore.

"That experience taught me every child is gifted, but it's up to the teachers to bring out that gift."

"By the time I was 19, I was quite mature," Ernestine said. "One day, I announced to my mother, 'I'm going to Africa,' and she said, 'Oh my gosh, look at you!' And I said, 'Mom you told me that I could do whatever I thought I was capable of doing, so...'"

"I was supposed to be there for only three weeks," Ernestine said, "but I ended up staying for three months. I kept going from country to country. People would stop me on the road and say, 'Would you like to come with us?' And I'm like, 'Sure.'" Ernestine even danced with the Enique Ali ballet and spent a month touring with them. She finally came home with several suitcases filled with gifts. But the greatest gift was that the trip to Africa reversed her life's direction...

"I didn't really have a childhood as such," Ernestine said. "I had been judged. Wrongly. I had been laughed at. But after that first trip to Africa it didn't matter anymore. That's what was beautiful about the whole thing: More than anything else— I proved to myself who I am."

And who Ernestine was, was a lifelong student and teacher. She still is.

Along her way, she ended up with four degrees, all Summa Cum Laude, as well as doing her doctoral work. "Really at the request of my mom," Ernestine said. "I mean four degrees what else do I need?"

Ernestine worked with U.S. Embassies around the globe developing curriculum and training teachers as well as opening new schools, which were primarily for the families of Americans who were serving overseas. She's been involved in education for the U.S. State Department for 12 years and has worked in 33 different countries.

"The reason I came back to America," Ernestine said, "was because my mom's doctor thought he'd discovered something alarming during her check-up. Mom was on her way to Alaska for a vacation, and I always told her make sure and have a little health exam before you travel."

Ernestine told her mom she was on her way back to Ghana anyway, so she'd be happy to stop in Florida and see her.

"When I got to the United States, I took her to the doctor. I was thinking I'd only be here for two weeks or so, but the doctor told us my mom had about two

95

and a-half months to live."

"If she only had two and a half months," Ernestine said, "by all means I wanted to be with her for that time." Ernestine had the Embassy send all her personal effects. She also had a big home in Ghana. So she sold her house and all the possessions she could, packed the rest and moved back to be with her mother.

"We travelled anywhere in the world my mother wanted to go for that first year," Ernestine said. "Then she started getting weak, so I took her to Germany to get alternative health care. I also took her to Mexico where she could get treatment she couldn't get here in the States."

Her mom lived for another three and a half years. By the time she passed away, Ernestine had spent all of her earnings and savings caring for and trying to keep her mother alive— $1.2 million in cash, and the proceeds from the sales of five homes and four pieces of land.

Now Ernestine was "dead broke" with no cash and no credit.

"I was destitute. I mean, I didn't have any funds coming in. I didn't have anything at all to pull from. I'd borrowed from friends, which I didn't want to do, but I had to keep the water on, the electricity, food..."

Ernestine had also developed fibromyalgia—a disorder characterized by widespread musculoskeletal pain accompanied by fatigue, sleep, memory and mood issues—so she simply couldn't work. The physical and financial pains were a debilitating combination, especially for an independent, active woman who'd never experienced either of those in her life before.

"I was talking to my doctor one day," Ernestine said. "Not only about my health, but my financial situation, too; asking what could I do? I was just so devastated. And I didn't realize that a lot of people were having difficulties with their credit at that time like me."

Her doctor was involved in a couple of Network Marketing companies, one of which was FDI—Financial Destination Inc., which she recommended to Ernestine, because she was a member herself and they helped people establish good credit.

Initially Ernestine had no interest in creating a business. She just wanted help with her finances. "But money showing up has a way of making people interested," Ernestine said, "especially when you are doggone broke." In a very short time, she began making money with her Network Marketing business, just by sharing with others what she was doing to help herself out financially.

"I said to myself, 'Well, you know what? You're not getting money from anywhere else. I guess you need to start doing this seriously.'" Ernestine was growing her business without really trying. "Mainly," she said, "because people trusted me, which speaks to the fact that relationships are what build a Network Marketing business."

"It's all about relationships: People caring about each other— understanding and being compassionate and just showing that you want to help."

"It's like when I went to my first convention," Ernestine said. "I was so excited to introduce myself to Bill Andreoli (Founder of FDI and now President of Youngevity) because I thought he was such a great guy. I put out my hand and said, 'Hi I'm Ernestine...' but he interrupted me saying, '...Ray, and you live in so and so, and you brought so and so people into the business.' And I was so surprised! I'm looking at him and I'm saying to myself, "Gosh is he the CIA?' He knew *everything* about me. But he just said, 'I know my winners.'"

"I still didn't quite know what I was doing. All I knew is I was bringing a lot of people on board. So I asked Bill could somebody help me? He introduced me to Dale Johnson. God bless him!" Ernestine said. "But he was so tough on me. And I'm like, *'I don't like this.'* One day I told Dale to stop yelling at me, and he said, 'Ernestine, I love you so much. I just want you to be successful,' and I got it. *I got it!*"

"I've worked with Presidents of countries when I was with the State Department. I've done so many things that I never thought I would do. I just had to go back and remember that I have been successful."

"I've learned and experienced that in every misfortune there is some fortune. You can use your challenges as stepping stones for the betterment of yourself," Ernestine said, "and it's never too late to bring about some positive change in your life."

"There's a saying that adversity introduces you to yourself."

"I had to learn to dream again," Ernestine said, "because when my mom died I felt like I just needed to die with her. I said to myself, 'Well, I'm not done. I'm going to dream and I will dream big. So I started dreaming big enough to achieve those things that I truly desired.'"

"I just started looking for the goodness in all things rather than thinking on the past negatives and just building on things that made my heart sing in those special moments and times. In fact, this is a special moment in time for Youngevity. We will never see this time again."

"My team's name is 'Team Legacy,' and that's my desire. If this was my last day on earth I just want to let it be known that I made a difference in the lives of many, many people."

"In Network Marketing we can leave an amazing legacy. Pulling others up. Lifting others up. I think it's so important."

"I don't think there is any other profession where you can do this so readily and with such great success."

"I think that Network Marketing is the answer," Ernestine said. "Where else are you going to go and be able to will every aspect of your business to future generations? I'm just so grateful to be in this space at this particular time and with such great people."

"Being in Network Marketing grows you as an individual and that helps you give more to society... Give more to mankind... And the more you give the more you will get.

"We have an opportunity here in Youngevity to build a legacy and to help people. I mean this is such a great time and we are making history every day even though we don't realize it. Youngevity is making history. We are making history right now, today."

"I know that Youngevity is in fact the place for me. It's my home. God has really laid His Hand on my life."

Ernestine Ray has a step-daughter Vivian, and she lives in Ft. Lauderdale, Florida, because, unlike New York where she grew up, Florida reminds her of Africa where it is never, ever cold.

A Little History

Richard Renton was born and raised in the Pacific North West —
and lives there to this day. His father was a successful banker in
Portland, Oregon, and his mother stayed home to raise their three
boys; James, John and Richard, who was the youngest. They were
a close-knit family, active in their community through the church,
scouting and sports.

Even with the challenges inherent growing up with three
competitive brothers, the Renton boys were very close. So it came
as a complete shock when John, only 17 years old, died of a brain
infection. It was an unwanted surprise to the family that Richard
said, "changes the structure of our lives forever."

"It got my attention to take life more seriously," he said. "I was
only 14, but I started to understand at that young age how fragile
our bodies are and how quickly things can change."

That understanding would become a beacon for Richard throughout his life.

Richard struggled with high school because he was dyslexic;
although back then the condition wasn't as understood nor even
acknowledged as it is today. "I had trouble reading. I had trouble
retaining information," Richard said. "But my parents' goal was to
get all their kids through college, so I entered the University of
Oregon in '73 and worked on my undergraduate degree in
physical education and health."

"I don't know if I was really mature enough where I should have
gone into a university right away. I struggled for my first few

years. I was active in sports in college, specifically baseball, but I had some setbacks with injuries," Richard said. "I blew my knee out."

Eventually, Richard finished college and moved up to Portland State University where he did post graduate work in sports medicine and became a Board Certified Athletic Trainer.

Richard worked for high schools and colleges including Portland State. He did his practicum work for the Portland Trailblazers, "Because you had to study underneath another trainer so many hours to become board certified," he said.

"What I realized in sports medicine is that the athletics trainer is either paid by the University or by the professional team, and their first concern really isn't the athlete, "Richard said.

"What I had in mind was that I would do everything I could do to promote health within the athlete, to help them take care of their body to the best that they could, so that they would have a long career," Richard said.

"But the team wants you on the field. Some organizations really don't care about the long term effects on athletes. Their big concern was, what can you do for me now, and that part was sad."

One of the ways Richard paid for college was to work in restaurants — either as a cook or a manager. That's where Richard got the bug to open his own business.

"I had an individual come to me and say we should open a salt water aquarium store," Richard said. "I've enjoyed pets throughout my life, so... I thought that was interesting." The banker's son took about 80 percent of his assets and invested in opening the store.

"I was the financier and my partner was supposed to be the one who knew how to take care of the fish and run the store," Richard said. "I realized he didn't have the knowledge he needed, so I went to all the other aquarium stores throughout Portland looking for someone to fill that role. I found this 17 year old, who knew more than just about every single owner out there."

"I proceeded to ask him: Would you A. Like to come work for me? (I told him I'd pay him more.) Or B. Become my partner?" Richard said. "He agreed to come to work and that first week, we became partners." His name was Steve Wallach.

What Richard says attracted him most to Steve was his knowledge, ability and desire to be a business owner.

An entrepreneur's first business typically fails. It took two or three years before that happened to Richard and Steve.

Then to earn some money quickly, they both became car salesmen— and in the process life-long friends.

Steve married Michelle— they met at the auto dealership— and Richard married Roxanne.

Steve and Michelle had begun working on a new project, a multi-level marketing company with Steve's dad called Soaring Eagle Ventures. The entrepreneurial couple was doing business from their living room and their garage. They asked Richard to join them. After two or three times asking, Richard finally said "Yes." As Roxanne was working and taking care of their bills, Richard was free to do "an experiment."

Steve's dad, Dr. Joel Wallach (Doc), was part owner of Soaring Eagle and had started giving his public health lectures across the country. Soon both couples had started earning half-way to six-figure a month incomes. Dr. Wallach began encouraging the company to make some of the products that he was recommending in his lectures, which nobody else was making, available but the company wasn't interested.

It was when the younger Wallach's and Renton's took a mini-vacation together that Michelle said, "Well, Richard, you know how to do that stuff."

So Steve, Richard, Michelle and Roxanne invested their own capital and started a company to provide the products to Doc's specifications.

Based on the persuasive power of Dr. Wallach and his tireless schedule of speaking events, they quickly started selling products faster than they could make them.

Then, for some inexplicably short-sighted reason, Soaring Eagle killed the golden egg. They terminated Dr. Wallach. That same day, they also "fired" Steve & Michelle and Richard & Roxanne. That immediately added hundreds-of-thousands of dollars per month to the company's profits, but in the process they'd signed their own death warrant. (Ironically, Soaring Eagle eventually became Supralife Network™, which was later acquired by Youngevity.)

"Doc basically went to his son and told him we need to have our own company. So we broke it down into sections," Richard said. "Doc continued to lecture, because what he does best is teaching people about diet and proper nutrition. Steve and Michele moved from Portland, Oregon, to San Diego, to set up the backbone of the business. I stayed up in Portland and started to develop the initial 12-15 products that Youngevity began with."

The new company was called American Longevity.

They were up and running, fully functioning in three months. That had never been done before in the history of Network Marketing.

It probably never will again.

Richard Renton relishes telling the story of Youngevity. And it's important to know that he isn't a paid corporate person. He's a Youngevity distributor growing his own Networking organization.

"Steve was a Network Marketer first before he was a company owner," Richard said. "We all were. So we understand what distributors go through. And when someone builds a business and is dependent on a company to supply products, and then all of a sudden the company starts to struggle, products aren't delivered or checks aren't paid... that reminds us of the challenges we had early in our careers."

"When we were Soaring Eagles," Richard said, "there was a lot of struggles with checks being late or they wouldn't even pay our commissions. The company would send us products instead and we would have to sell them to get our money. So our intention was to build a quality product line and pay commissions and never be late." And they never have.

"Steve's dream, his passion, is to get his dad's word out," Richard said. "Well, the whole idea of MLM is word-of-mouth marketing. So we get a team, then an army, and then a crusade to get Doc

Wallach's word out about 90 for LIFE and how dramatically the right nutrition can change people's lives."

"Dr. Wallach and his passion, his love for his mission, is the cornerstone of the company," Richard said. "I think every distributor that's involved with Youngevity, every customer that takes a Youngevity product owes thanks to him for his determination, desire and his drive to get the message out there."

"Doc talks about living to 100. I can't imagine the man not living to 100, because he has more energy than I have and *he's 14 years older than I am!*" Richard said.

"He is out there speaking 300 days a year. He's on the radio for two hours a day, five days a week; he's traveling and doing all those things just to get the word out."

"I look back as I was raised and I was blessed to have two parents throughout my whole life, and my mother got to be a stay at home mom. We always sat down and had dinner together," Richard said. "I mean always, always, always."

"You look at the new generation now... most of the time both parents are working. A common dinner might be McDonalds. And we don't spend as much time talking and communicating. I think that's something we are losing as a society and I think Multi-Level Marketing can give that back to us."

"It's real easy for you to recommend a restaurant if you like a restaurant. It's real easy for you to recommend a movie if you like a movie. This business gives you an opportunity to recommend a product if you like it and then it's your customer's choice whether they want to take advantage of it. The difference is *you get paid for it.*

"Youngevity gives people a chance to have their own business where they can put as little or as much time into it as they want and have a chance to be successful," Richard said. "It gives people the opportunity to have an at-home job, so that they can choose when they work and they can choose the goals they want to reach and spend more quality time with their family."

"That's why I love it."

Richard lives with the love of his life, his wife Roxanne, in the place he loves most, Washougal, Washington, located on the Columbia River. Washougal sits at the west entrance to the Columbia River Gorge with a view of snow-capped Mount Hood rising above the Cascade Mountains. Richard and Roxanne have a son, Shanon, who is 42 years old.

Change Your Mind

Todd Smith started life in Portland, Oregon. He was the first born to a struggling dental student and his wife; who started out living in government housing. Eventually, Todd's sister and two brothers joined the family.

As his father's lifestyle and income increased, Todd realized there were a lot of things he'd gone through as a child that helped form his perceptions and understanding of life that his siblings didn't get to experience.

> **"I'm grateful for that," Todd said, "because I think I have a bit of a different perspective that helped me when I started my own family."**

"As a kindergartener and first grader I loved the fact that every year we'd do a field trip where I'd get to walk from my school with all my classmates and we'd go on a tour of my dad's dental practice. I thought I was the king of the world. That was really great."

"Those first few years were pretty lean." Todd said. "I remember my parents would budget and decide whether it was school clothes or food or saving for a family car. There was a lot more of that going on back then than there was later as my dad's practice grew."

"I actually grew up on a farm," Todd said. "My dad owned some property and he had us work in the garden, in the fields and the orchard all the time. We would grow all this food, harvest it and can it or put it in the root cellar. We'd eat off of that all winter. We weren't poor. It was just my dad putting every penny towards paying off the house and his debts."

As a young boy, Todd started playing ice hockey and fell in love with it. Todd's coach told him, "You can accomplish anything you put your mind to." The coach even had that phrase stuck to his refrigerator in his home. Todd asked him if he *really* believed it. The coach answered, "Absolutely. I don't question it at all. Ever."

You can be and do anything you put your mind to.

Todd thought, "Wow. I don't really know if *I* believe it, but sure enough Coach does." Todd remembers asking his dad about it. His father said, "Look, you can do things you never dreamed of if you set your mind to it and are willing to pay the price."

Todd went through a difficult time in junior high school— he was pretty depressed and he'd distanced himself from all his friends. He walked around in a big down parka with his face hidden deep inside the hood. The teachers knew something was wrong, and Todd's parents became very concerned.

One day his dad said, "Todd, I've got an idea." He knew that Todd was playing tennis and he knew Todd really wanted to make it to first string on the team. He also knew Todd *really* wanted to beat Chad Olsen, the number one player, but he just wasn't good enough— yet.

"My dad knew, and he said, 'Todd I've got a deal for you.'" His father told him they were joining the tennis club. (Even though he'd told Todd before, "There's no way we can put that kind of money out for tennis.") His dad said, "We'll play tennis for 45 minutes every morning and then I'll drop you off at school." Teenager that he was, Todd wasn't at all excited about getting up *that* early. "I'd really rather been sleeping," Todd admitted.

But he wanted to join that club so badly he said, "Dad, absolutely. Let's do it."

"On the way there and back," Todd said, "my dad would play these cassette tapes: *See You at the Top* by Zig Ziglar. I didn't really care for Zig's Yazoo Mississippi accent, nor his strange stories, but I got to play tennis and that's all that mattered."

One day, his dad said, "Todd, you know those tapes that I listen to when we're in the car? Well, I've got some friends that need to hear them, but I only have the one set. If I paid you, would you make copies for me so I could share them with those people?" Todd said, "Sure."

"He got me a dubbing machine, but it wasn't high speed," Todd said. "I had to listen to each one while I was copying to make sure I heard when the side ended, so I could flip it over. My dad was paying me $0.50 a cassette tape and I wanted to get as many done as I could."

"While I was studying, while I was playing basketball, while I was playing soccer, whatever I was doing, I'd carry this little machine around with me and I'd be making copies of those tapes."

Skip forward 25 years later. Todd is married with kids of his own, his parents just sold their home and Todd's helping them move. "I'm cleaning out the closet in my dad's office," Todd said, "and you know what I found? All those tapes I made. Every one. Still boxed up. Labels an' all. He never gave them to anyone."

"You can change who you are. You can change wherever you are by changing what goes into your mind," Todd said. "If you're not happy with anything in your life,

change your mind."

"Thanks to my dad," Todd said, "that's engrained in me."

Todd went on to college and chose his major based on what was most popular at the time, and what would keep the most doors open for his future. So he got a degree in accounting, but... he didn't really enjoy it. Speaking with a number of his father's friends, Todd asked, "Was there one thing you wished you'd studied?" Every one of them said, "I wish I had more background in law." So Todd enrolled in law school.

During his first year of Law school, Todd and his wife spent more than $40,000 for three years of treatments and doctors' appointments trying to have children. Finally, they were successful. "We were elated," Todd said, "because doctor after doctor had told us we'd never have our own children. So of course you can imagine our excitement when we found out we were having *triplets!*"

At a meeting for the support group, the Triplet Connection, Todd came face-to-face with the reality of life with three-at-once. A man came up to him after and said, "So are you ready for having the triplets?" Todd told him about the triple-stroller he'd bought, the great cribs he'd gotten a line on and... The man interrupted and said, "No. Are you *really* ready; time-wise, physically, financially, emotionally?"

"Honestly, I don't know," Todd said. And it was an *honest* answer. He didn't have a clue."

Todd didn't really know until Jessica, Cassidy and McCall were born. He promptly found himself "in a funk." Trying to keep up with school, a full-time job, lack of sleep, needing help from both sides of the family. "It was overwhelm in the extreme."

"I was forced to make a choice," Todd said. "I'm either going to have to drop out of school, or I'm going to have to quit my job. I can't do both— *and* I was needed at home, *all* the time. I've got to be able to finish my education *and* I've got to provide for my family. How do I do both?"

Todd made the hard decision. He quit his job.

He knew he had to find another way to earn income, one that was flexible enough for him to remain in school, but... He quickly ran out of viable options, so he went to speak to his father.

"Once my dad recovered from me telling him that I was quitting my job, we talked" Todd said. "I told him the ideas I'd found; assembly at the home, medical billing, collection. Then he told me about my mom who'd had heel spurs and arthritis and wasn't sleeping well and had night cramps. He talked about the injury in his shoulder."

"Your mom... her heel spurs are gone. Her arthritis is gone. Her leg cramps are gone. My shoulder," his dad said. "I couldn't carry anything and now look..." And he swung his arm round and round in a big circle."

"We got hooked up with this veterinarian turned people doctor," Todd's father said. "We've been taking his stuff and its done wonders for us. You ought to go talk to the friends we buy it from to see if there's any way you can get involved selling Dr. Wallach's products."

Todd was 26 years old and had never heard of Network Marketing before.

"I was driving back home and I popped in the cassette they'd given me, *Dead Doctors Don't Lie.* All of a sudden I thought, 'I've got to buy this stuff.' And my next thought was, 'A-ha! I'll just get people to listen to this *Dead Doctors...* tape, and the ones that are interested will go and buy it.'" That's how Todd got started — and to this day, that's how he shares Doc Wallach's message of 90 For Life with people.

One day, Todd's neighbor, who'd signed up in another Network Marketing company, came to him said, 'I need your help. I've got a man coming to my house and who's going to do a presentation and I've got to fill the room. Would you come and be one of the guests?'"

Todd agreed and went. The speaker was late, and when he finally came in he just started right into his presentation. Todd recognized him.

"Hold on," he said. "That's Blake Graham." They had been roommates in college as freshmen.

After the meeting Blake asked Todd, "What are you doing here?" Todd said, "I'm in Network Marking. I'm with Dr. Joel Wallach's new company."

Blake said, "You mean *THE* Dr. Wallach?" Todd said, "That's the one." Blake said, "What do you mean he's starting a new company?" Todd said, "This is actually his own company now."

"Blake seemed so skilled and knowledgeable," Todd said. "I told him, 'I need your expertise and your knowledge. I've got a vehicle that I know will fly, but I need help.' The two formed a partnership there-and-then and they've climbed to the very top of Youngevity together.

"The million-dollar-plus income earners I think we can learn the most," Todd said, "are like Blake: People who have consistently, over an extended period of time, taken the small steps and done the small actions to share the message, improve themselves and help to improve others."

"Much like Dr. Wallach, the mission, the purpose of what they are doing is bigger than any of the bumps in the road," Todd said. "One way or another they'll find their way over, under, around or through whatever stands in front of them. They cannot be shaken."

"They know if they just continue those small consistent efforts over time, the law of averages is in their favor and they're going to end up on top."

"Because of my upbringing and my education," Todd said. "I think I could have found another profession. But I don't believe I could ever have received anywhere near the level of personal satisfaction of helping so many people that Network Marketing has given me."

"It's great to see how you can be involved with something that helps you pay your bills, change your life financially, give you freedom and at the same time make you a better person when all is said and done," Todd said.

"The joy that comes when I see people change their lives by changing their minds. That's my greatest reward."

Todd Smith lives in Alpine, Utah, with his wife Darcie and their eight girls: the threesome of Jessica, Cassidy and McCall, and Ellie, Avory, Adelaide, Islay and Emberly, who just turned 1 year old.

The Freedom Is Priceless

Rich Stocks was born in Poplar Bluff, Missouri, and with the exception of seven years away, he's lived there his entire life. And he started out his life extremely poor.

"I'll tell you how poor I was," Rich said. "In my early adult years I was working at this church. I was looking on the wall at the government income guidelines to qualify for the food we got from the church. And I looked at the row along the bottom that said 'poverty' and I didn't qualify."

Rich's mother worked in a factory for 30 years — until the factory closed leaving her with a "whopping" pension of $124 and some change every month. His father was the custodian for the local high school in Poplar Bluff. He worked there for 37 years until he retired, and then still kept working there as much as they would let him; up until the time that he passed away. "So, I was poor," Rich said.

"I was an only child. I really never felt poor. I never went hungry. I never went without proper clothing. My dad would drive cars until he drove them to death. That was a little embarrassing when they would pick me up at school or at the movie in this old ratty car, but I didn't *feel* poor. I was a pretty independent minded kid."

> **"I don't ever remember my parents talking much to me about college, or grades, or 'did you do your homework?' I guess I was pretty self-motivated— and quite the dreamer."**

The Freedom Is Priceless

"I remember when I was in elementary school we would go to the checkout line at the grocery store," Rich said, "and I would want to get the magazines with the big fancy homes and mansions."

"I was a dreamer. I have no idea where I got that from, because my parents were content with where they were. I just wasn't willing to grow up in those same conditions."

Rich did well in school. Not top of his class, but he was an honor student. "Both my parents only finished 8th grade," Rich said. "But my mother would read to me every night. Perhaps that's where I developed a love for learning. I always looked forward to the book mobile and if it wasn't my turn to go I would say to the other kids, 'Hey get this book and that for me...' because I wanted to just read them all."

Rich started college while he was still in high school. He'd start and stop, and start and stop again. Just a few years ago he went back and finished a degree he started when he was 18. "It took me almost 30 to complete a four-year degree," he said. "But I got it done."

Rich ended up majoring in Psychology, which he says is "the lowest paying of all the 4 year degrees." He was genuinely interested in how the mind works; the thinking process. He was also intrigued by criminology, and he went to Bible School, which was in addition to his secular education.

"That was part of that seven years when I moved away from Poplar Bluff," Rich said. "It was a great experience. I had the secular education in psychology and then the ministry training as well."

In Rich's first full year in college he was introduced to Network Marketing.

"My wife and I— she wasn't my wife then but we were engaged to be married about a year or so later— we were looking in the help wanted section of a local newspaper," Rich said. "I don't remember what the ad said, but someone had disguised their Network Marketing opportunity as a regular help wanted ad."

Rich thought he was going for a job interview. He found himself knocking on the door of a local hotel and a lady opened the door. She was very friendly with an extreme southern accent and said, "Come on in." Rich started to feel weird right away.

"Her husband was seated behind a little table," Rich said, "and he stood up and shook my hand. To be honest, I was not comfortable at all *and* I sure wasn't happy. I thought I'd been tricked. Deceived. He got out a flip chart and started giving me a presentation."

One of the first questions the man asked Rich was had he ever heard of Multilevel Marketing? Rich hadn't. He was just 19.

The man said "Surely you've heard of Amway?" but Rich heard Amtrak. "Maybe I'm applying for a job on the rail road," Rich thought.

"So he's going through the flip chart presentation and I'm sitting there and to be honest," Rich said, "I'm looking at it, but I'm ignoring him. I can't wait until it's over. I just want to get out of there. I'm trying to be friendly, but..."

"But then he got to the part with the circles," Rich said. "When I saw the circles... You know what I mean; the top circle had the word YOU, which was me. Underneath that was another circle. Bob. You introduce Bob to this product, this service. Every time Bob uses it you get paid. And underneath that was another circle. Every time he uses the product or service you get paid. And there was another circle... and another."

119

"You're a kid who'd grown up poor and now you're looking at these circles and dollar-signs. He had my attention then," Rich said. "My full attention."

"I thought, 'There are only four people in the world that know about this; this guy and his wife in that hotel room, and me and whoever invented created this idea.' That's really what I thought," Rich said. "Not only that, but I thought when I walked out of this room no one who sees this will ever say no!"

"I just knew I was going to be rich by this time next week."

And of course, reality slapped Rich in the face shortly after, but Rich joined that company. He went out and he started working hard and within a week the FDA took their product off the market. The company went on to become a giant and still is today, but Rich didn't recover.

"They put me out of business," Rich said, "but I thought, well I'll try again. I believed in the circles." Rich tried a number of "circles," more than a dozen, but nothing worked. "MLM stood for 'Massive Loss of Money,'" Rich said. "And I was in the NFL. That's where you have *No Friends Left*. I finally just said the words, 'Never again.'"

Rich stuck with that "Never again" vow for 10 years. He absolutely *hated* Network Marketing.

"One day someone called," Rich said, "and they didn't have that funny sales sound in their voice. They just said, 'Rich we've heard this amazing cassette tape — veterinarian, physician, live to be 100.' They didn't tell me the name of it. They were not in a company. They weren't selling anything. They didn't know anything about

Rich Stocks

the product. I said 'Hmm.' It piqued my interest a little bit, but I said, 'I don't want to listen to that.'"

Here's where Rich's story starts to become stranger than fiction. "Before the week was out," Rich said, "somebody from another state called me."

> **"They didn't have the funny sound in their voice. They told me they heard this amazing cassette tape— veterinarian, physician, live to be 100.' They didn't tell me the name of it. They were not in a company..."**

"You've got the idea. But I still refused to listen."

At that time Rich was pastoring a church, and one of the ladies in his parish had her business right behind the church. "I'm back in the corner of her office one day making copies, and a very wealthy business man walked through the door. He and I had never met," Rich said, "but everybody in town knew him. He walked in and said, 'I heard this cassette tape, veterinarian, physician, live to be 100...' And I heard this eerie sound that used to be on the Twilight Zone TV show. I just could not believe I'm hearing about this cassette tape thing— *from him,* and again— *three times that week!"*

Rich decided right then and there, somebody, somewhere was trying to get something good into his hands. So he went back to that first person who contacted him and said, "Hey I'll listen to that cassette tape now." Five minutes into the audio Rich learned it was Dr. Joel Wallach's "Dead Doctors Don't Lie."

"When I heard the cassette it so moved me. It was just so powerful," Rich said. "I thought everyone on the planet needs to hear this message!"

At the time, there were more than 50 different companies sending out the "Doctor's Don't Lie" cassettes, and it took a while for Rich to find Dr. Wallach's own company. That was May of 1997, and the company had only just started in April. Finding the company created two problems for Rich. First, it was Network Marketing — and he'd sworn "Never again." The other problem, Rich was so broke he didn't have the $6 to join, much less purchase products.

"I didn't know what to do," Rich said. "How are you going to tell your wife when you said you'd never do Network Marketing again? But the message won out."

Now... about that $6.

Rich found a number of people who'd also gotten "Dead Doctors..." tapes and he rounded up as many copies as he could. He soaked and soaped the labels, scraped them off with a butter knife and scribbled his own name and phone number on the cassettes and began loaning them out to everyone he knew.

"I had one goal," Rich said. "I wanted to get his products. I had to have them. So I'm going to do enough business to get mine free. That's my only goal."

Rich did just that. First, he made $100 a month. Then $200. He kept doing that until the end of the first year, when he was making as much as a full-time worker in Poplar Bluffs would have made. At the end of two years, Rich was earning a six-figure income.

"And I've received a paycheck from Dr. Wallach every month for 17 years now," Rich said. "I've never missed a month, never been paid late and I've never had a check bounce. I have to pinch myself sometimes to make sure that it's real."

"With Youngevity we offer people health freedom, financial freedom and time freedom. You need all three of those for a happy life. But to me," Rich said, "the biggest one of all is that time freedom."

"I decided long ago that I didn't want someone telling me what time to show up for work, what time I can go home, what time I could use the bathroom, what time I could eat my lunch and all of those things."

"To me that's prison. That's bondage."

"The freedom is priceless. The freedom to come and go and do what we want when we want."

"The word freedom just means the absence of restraint, unrestricted, and that's what I like most about this business — that flexibility. I work, but I work when I want. You cannot put a price tag on that."

"I can say now, as a guy who once hated Network Marketing, that I absolutely love it. It just doesn't get any better than this. The freedom I have is priceless."

Rich Stocks still lives in Poplar Bluff, Missouri with his wife Dee and two of their four children, Jessica, who's 28 and Christopher 17 and in his last year of high school. Their two other children are Elizabeth 26 and David 25, and when David graduates, "Who knows..." Rich says.

The Perfect Storm

Michelle Van Etten was born and raised in Vero Beach, Florida. It's a place most people don't know exists until a tropical storm or hurricane hits, which, astonishingly, happens on average every two-and-a-half years. Hurricane Francis did its beach-leveling best to wipe Vero Beach off the map in 2004.

By that time, Michelle had been gone for six years. Michelle's parents have been together for 42 years now, so she grew up with a mom and dad who loved and would do anything for each other. They were educated people and Michelle said, "Their big thing was always a push for us— my two brothers and I— to go to college. 'You have to go to college. You have to go to college.' It was the typical American working dream. Get into a good school, go to college… then go on to the real world. That's what they had planned for me."

But 5' 11" green-eyed, blonde Michelle Barnett had other plans. By age 13, she wanted to model.

"When I was 16, I had a chance to go to New York (if my parents would let me) and be one of the Top Ten Teen models," Michelle said. "That was *way* more interesting and exciting to me than school. But since I wasn't getting the kind of grades you need for a scholarship, I realized I needed to get a job instead."

"I wasn't the best at the work thing, so I had multiple jobs,"

Michelle said. "I ended up graduating from high school with medium grades, nothing spectacular. Then I went to a community college and it took about six years to get a two-year degree, because I was working the whole time."

Michelle found a love for bartending and she ended up doing that for 13 years. That's how she put herself through school. While working on her Bachelor's degree she fell in love with psychology.

"I was being fast tracked for my Masters and Bachelors at the same time," Michelle said, "because I had excelled in school—I think I needed those six years to grow up— so finally I figured out what I wanted to do."

In her senior year of college, Michelle met her husband Jimmy and 11 months later they were married. Nine days later she discovered she was pregnant.

Michelle had to make a decision. She was going to be a mom... School was two hours away... What's the best way forward?

"I actually never used my degree," Michelle said. "Except I guess I use it every day now. That psychology background, being able to talk to people and get a feel for what they are going through, who they are and how I can help, was great preparation for Network Marketing."

Michelle's circumstances led her to becoming an entrepreneur, working from home. "I designed different things on ceiling fans, from sports memorabilia to everything under the sun," Michelle said. "I made over 1100 ceiling fans in a year and a-half. Eventually I got bored with that, but I knew at that point

I couldn't work for somebody else."

One day, Michelle discovered scrapbooking— it kept her sane while she was taking care of a toddler. *That* became a *very* expensive hobby. "I think I spent about $10,000 *very quickly*," she said. "I knew I had to do something to support my hobby-habit, so

126

I started working on creating design projects for manufacturers, because then they would send me free products."

Immediately, Michelle found herself working for nine different companies; creating products and projects for them to put in their magazines, books or for displays in stores and trade shows. She worked her way up the ladder very quickly.

"I started going to the different exhibitions, like the Crafts & Hobby show," Michelle said. "I worked the booths for manufacturers and I happened to work for the very best of the best in the business. I was able to visit France, Italy, Australia, Germany, Holland, the Bahamas. I traveled for Canon, because I made friends with the person who was in charge of all of their advertising and marketing." Michelle did that for 10 years.

"One day," Michelle said, "I realized my 20-year high school reunion was coming up. So I went online to check out the girls I'd gone to school with. I was thinking, 'Oh yeah. Well, they're all moms now, so....' Wow! They looked like Barbies — *and* they were all driving BMW's! I'm like, 'What is going on?' How did these single moms with two kids, afford to look like they do and drive those cars?"

"I wanted to look like Barbie and drive a BMW too."

And that's how Michelle found her first Network Marketing company.

"I re-connected with a girl that I went to school with," Michelle said. "She was as crazy as the day is long, but I started working with her. (Not the best choice I could have made.) I had no clue what I was doing, but I had a burning desire, especially once I started understanding a little more about leveraged income."

"I was already an online person. I had an eBay business from back in the ceiling fan day. So, when I saw that I could do Network Marketing that way... Well, I just dominated that area. I was doing extremely, *extremely* well and my lifestyle changed completely, quickly."

"I soon had a BMW convertible. My husband had a brand new truck. We bought a new boat. Quite a few other things along the way. And then, one day," Michelle said, "they just pulled the rug out from underneath me and things started going downhill *fast!*"

"I had taught my team to do online sales," Michelle said. "And out of the blue, even though it was in the policies, they changed it. And when they did, they changed it so much they cut it all out completely."

"All of a sudden $4,000 or $5,000, even $8,000 monthly incomes were $200 or $300. That was a really hard blow," Michelle said. "I learned that you've got to really protect yourself and your people. Now I understand, you've got to support your team in a way that they will work no matter what."

> **"I was so green. I didn't know anything. I didn't know how to train people or how to create that kind of bond that's required for lasting success in Network Marketing."**

"I begged the company to take another look at their policies," Michelle said. "I begged them to change, so that new people coming in wouldn't have those issues. It was just not a playing field that was working. They said, 'No.'"

"One of my friends had kept contacting me about another company, and finally one day I was ready to listen."

"Happy people don't leave, their company. Period. If you are happy," Michelle said, "you're not going to be seeking some other place. You're not going to be looking. If you are really happy where you are, nothing will pull you away." Michelle was very unhappy and left to join her second company. Everything looked great on the outside, but something just didn't feel right to her. She tried. She gave it everything she had. But it didn't work.

So Michelle decided to go to an industry event offered by The Association of Network Marketing Professionals to learn more. Michelle didn't know why she felt so compelled to attend. She just knew she had to be there. "I hadn't even asked my husband about going nor bought a plane ticket," Michelle said.

Only two weeks before the event, Michelle finally told Jimmy he had to buy her ticket. So, even though things were pretty tight he bought it. But then, she made him change it, so she wouldn't miss the Friday Sessions. "I *had* to be there," she said.

"I couldn't tell him why. I didn't even understand it myself. I'm like, 'Trust me, honey. I just have to be there.'" So Jimmy changed Michelle's ticket and that Friday, Michelle met industry legend Keith Halls. "He's my mentor and my friend, and I'm so blessed to be able to work with him." Keith got up on stage and he told his story. For Michelle, "He was speaking right to my soul."

She *had* to meet Keith. To get to know him, and hopefully work with him one day.

"Now that I know Keith," Michelle said, "I think I was being interviewed. He was making sure I was the type of person he'd want to work with, that I had the characteristics that he looks for. We talked and we started becoming friends. We would speak back and forth quite frequently along the way and he told me he was up to something, but didn't tell me what."

"He's like, 'When I'm ready I will tell you, I promise.' So that was March. In May he sent me a text: 'Are you available tomorrow?' I wrote back, 'Yes, of course. Anytime.' I told my husband 'I know we are in dire straits, but whatever Keith's into I want to do it. I know he is somebody I'm supposed to work with.'"

Keith had spent two-and-a-half years looking for the right company. When he found Youngevity, he called Michelle right away.

"I had no reservations," Michelle said. "None. I had such a belief in who I would be working with. When I really did my research — because I'm a researcher — I fell in love with every aspect of Youngevity: So many different products to choose from. Dr. Wallach's message. I went to work immediately. Keith and his partner Cody McKinley were moving at the speed of light. They got in April and were already almost at the top and I wasn't letting them out of my sights." Cody told Michelle, "You have no clue who you are. You don't realize what you can do and what you *could* be and *will* be. I know. I've seen it before. You just have to tap into it."

He was right. And Michelle tapped in big time. How?

"Think and Grow Rich," Michelle said. "Having a burning desire, a purpose that you are not willing under any circumstances to second guess. Your definite purpose has got to be there, laser focused."

"If you know what you want, nothing can stand in your way. You have to believe it. I believed — as crazy as this was — one of my goals was to 'retire' my husband. Life was pretty good for us, so that would be quite a risk, but I believed and Youngevity gave me the way."

Jimmy retired on March 21st, 2014.
As Michelle said, when you believe,
nothing can stand in your way.

"I have a passion to see people succeed," Michelle said. "I pride myself on teaching others to pay it forward, to always be recruiting to help their teams grow. I brought on five CEOs this month and I placed those people under my new people to help them move up in rank. Creating leaders is the key — and always doing whatever it takes to help your people succeed."

"We are in the right place with the right company, the right product... everything. You have the right people. You have the integrity. You have the company that has the right heart. There is passion, there is belief, there is truth here. And the truth really will set you *financially* free."

"It's like the perfect storm," Michelle said. "And in every perfect storm there is that one great wave and you want to be on it and ride it. Paddle as far and as fast as you can, because you don't want to miss it. I don't want *you* to miss it. We are just getting started. We are just now coming into the wave."

"Three years from now it's going to be insane."

———————————————

Michelle Van Etten and her retired husband Jimmy, have two children: James 11 and Malia who's 7. They live in Valrico, on the west coast of Florida, where there aren't so many hurricanes.

The Movie of Your Life

Andre Vaughn grew up in Baltimore, Maryland, in a family of five: Mother, father, an older brother, Lenard, whom he looked up to "dearly," and his twin sister Andrea, who was his best friend — when they weren't fighting with each other.

"We grew up in sports," Andre said. "We were always competing against each other. I really believe that helped set us up for later on in life. We were always active in every type of sports all throughout school. We were athletes, we were competitive and we were born leaders."

"The best thing was we had a loving household," Andre said. "My parents had a couple of difficulties and eventually they decided to separate, but going through high school we kept it together no matter what. When you're not used to certain things, you have to rise up and you've got to be courageous to get things done."

Andre said he graduated not "Magna Cum Laude" but "Thank You, Laude."

He was so glad to, "Grab that diploma and just get out of there!" Andre had to go to a pre-college program in order to be accepted by a University. "My sister, of course, was accepted without doing any of that. Ahhh," Andre said, "the joy— and pressure— of having a very smart twin sister."

"One of the major things I realized," Andre said, "and I'd tell my mom: I'd say, 'Listen, I've got to stay in *my* lane. It doesn't matter that she got straight A's. That doesn't mean anything. That's her race and I'm going to run mine.'" As Andre said, the Vaughn children were competitors.

Ulitmately, Andre joined his sister and got into the University of Maryland at Eastern Shore. He says he learned much more from the experience of being there on his own, than from the classes he took.

"When I got there I joined a fraternity," Andre said, "and I got in to a few 'situations' that forced me to sit out for a semester. While I was on 'vacation' from college I remember my parents constantly telling me, 'We are only going to *one* graduation.'"

So there he was, a full semester behind his straight-A sister, remembering what his parents kept saying about *only going to one graduation*. Andre took it seriously.

"I was determined I was going to do whatever I needed to get out of there and graduate with my sister," Andre said. "I had 21 credits, then 24 credits; winter session, summer session... Needless to say, even though I had to sit out for a semester, my sister and I graduated on time and together."

"I really believe that was the point in my life where I realized when I put my mind to something, it is already done."

When Andre got out of college, he decided he wanted to be a lawyer. He'd graduated in December and thought he needed to make some money before the fall. So he started teaching second grade. To this day he's still amazed he ended up doing that: "I loved those kids," Andre said, "Didn't love the money at all, but loved the kids and enjoyed what I did."

Andre then decided to get his Master's degree so he could earn more money. But when he finished his Master's at the University of Maryland, he started asking, "Man, what in the world am I doing? Teaching? I love nice things and I can't afford them, and the other teachers can't afford them either." Andre realized he needed to do something different — something very different.

One day in Church he heard the message, "If you want to walk on water you've got to get off the boat." It was time for Andre to get off the boat.

"I just did it cold turkey. I quit teaching." Andre said. He opened up a mortgage company and almost immediately he opened up a real estate company, too. "I ended up having 40 agents that worked for me," Andre said. "And here's the crazy part: I figured out that I could own a real estate company without being a real-estate broker. So, I hired the brokers to *work for me!*"

Andre started that company, brought on some amazing partners and they grew fast and big. They did real estate investments, helped individuals buy homes, and worked commercial deals as well. They had fun and they were successful, but real estate was becoming quite a roller coaster ride. Andre wanted more – more upside, and more time freedom.

One day, a childhood friend who trained horses came to Andre and said, "I want you to buy a horse."

Andre knew nothing about horses — just as he once knew nothing about real estate and mortgages. He'd proven you didn't have to be an expert to make money in any endeavor. "You just have to be willing, to be coachable and have a positive mindset," Andre said. "So I decided to give that guy a try and bought a horse. It felt really good."

The first time Andre's horse went out, it came in fifth place. Although he was *in the money*, Andre didn't like fifth place. He was used to winning. So he immediately put that horse back in a higher stakes race, and even though it was on a "blackout" day, that horse ran and won in front of 100,000 people!

Andre had just gotten a taste of the good life. And, he wanted more.

"I probably won over 20 races with different horses," Andre said. "It was really a beautiful thing. I simply applied the same principles that I did in mortgage, and real estate, and in my own life. With that positive mindset and a winning attitude, knowing that you don't have to be the expert... You can be ignorance on fire, instead of knowledge on ice. And fire wins, every time! However," Andre continued, "you're only as good as the last horse, in your last race..."

While he was still involved in horse racing, Dr. Willie Richardson introduced Andre to Network Marketing.

"He called me and told me about the concept," Andre said. "And I said, 'Man I've always wanted to meet you and work with you, but I just never found that right company for me." Dr. Richardson told Andre he'd finally found the right one: Financial Destination, Inc. — FDI for short— founded by William Andreoli. "And man," Andre said, "it was just a beautiful ride right away."

"It took me about six months to make a six-figure income. It was so right, because the real estate market was great and FDI offered financial services," Andre said. "It just went hand in hand with all the things we'd already done."

"I got my first chance to actually build a team. I went through the ranks in record time at FDI," Andre said. "It was just a great thing and I learned a lot." But more importantly, he learned what *not* to do.

136

"We went so fast starting out it was scary. It got to the point where we were making a lot of bad decisions, because everybody who was in my upline was brand new, too. So nobody really had the secret," Andre said. "We were running on sheer excitement."

"You really need the fundamentals," Andre said, "because excitement doesn't last. We ran that enthusiasm up as far as we could until we had to start learning the principles and the basics of the business."

Andre was the first person to achieve Presidential Marketing Director at FDI. He was also the first person to get to Vice Chairman Marketing Director. "It was good," he said. "I got various awards and they presented me with checks that I hadn't made in two years of teaching second grade."

"One of the major mistakes I made," Andre said, "was I built a welfare system. When I recruited people I would put people under them. It made it so everybody was dependent on me and although they hit the achievement ranks they were really paper champions."

Andre realized he wasn't building a solid structure. Even though the organization had gotten big, fast, it could grow no further. "It wasn't really Network Marketing as it was supposed to be," he said, "based on a simple duplicatable system everyone could follow."

"I almost felt like I owned a job instead of a business," Andre said. "In fact, my 'job' really owned me. That's not why I got into Network Marketing."

"One reason for that was I just didn't seek out true mentorship," Andre said. "So I went back to my sponsor, Dr. Willie Richardson.

He taught me how to conduct myself, how to carry myself, and how to deal with people no matter what."

"And Mr. William Andreoli, really started teaching me about the business. He spent some quality time with me. I knew I could trust his word," Andre said, "and that he could really shape me and mold me into the business leader I needed to become."

"One of the things he taught me was to always know the situation you are in: Know the reps you're dealing with, know your people. He taught me about setting folks up for success, not failure, and helping people to get out of their own way and letting folks lead."

"And he taught me to be excited when you have folks doing just a little bit, because some people's little bit can be much more than other folks' 100 percent."

"He taught me to get folks doing money-making activities, and to look at your cash register on a daily basis like multi-million dollar businesses do. I'm forever grateful for that mentorship," Andre said.

"The greatest thing I tell people that I've learned is how to dance in the storm — and there will be storms," Andre said. "I always try to keep a positive mindset. I know I'm building momentum all around me, so when people are looking at the negative I'm always looking at the positive. I'm always trying to take the high road and take it one step at a time."

"Being positive and being genuinely willing to help people — that's a major thing with me," Andre said. "Just really caring about people and going to the next level with them no matter what's happening with me... No matter what's happening with them either."

"And then there's my family's support," Andre said. "That's such a great thing to have — a family that supports what you do. And having an extended family that supports what you do, too — your Network Marketing family. And having a mentor like Bill Andreoli. I know with all of that support I can be the best person I can possibly be."

"And I really believe my relationship with God is number one," Andre said. "That's *the* key to my success."

"Network Marketing is all in the relationships," Andre said. "I never would have had these relationships being a second grade school teacher. Or in real estate, mortgages, horse racing. I would have never bumped into Bill Andreoli. The relationship that you can earn from folks really builds you up. Network Marketing is like a built-in personal development program where you are growing as a leader constantly."

"And your income is only going to grow at your level of development. Your income is unlimited in Network Marketing," Andre said.

"Your growth as a person, as a leader, is unlimited in this business. That's why we say you can write your own paycheck."

"In Network Marketing it's your movie. I'm making the movie of my life, right here, right now. And it's going to be a great, inspirational movie," Andre said. "It already is."

Andre Vaughn lives with his wife Monique and their four year old twin girls, Londyn and Logan in Baltimore, Maryland, where he is producing, directing, writing and staring in the movie of his life.

Thank You Money

Nephi Wayman was born and raised on a small family farm on the west side of the county just outside of Salt Lake City, Utah. He grew up raising animals; feeding cows, pigs, chickens and tending gardens. "We did a lot of work as we were quite poor growing up," Nephi said. "But we were very happy. I absolutely look back on it with longing, because it was such a great childhood. We were busy, but it was a lot of fun."

Nephi didn't know his family was poor. It was only when the neighbor kids would come over and they had "bakers' bread" bought from the store, while Nephi had homemade bread that his momma made. And they would have baloney on their sandwiches and Nephi would have peanut butter or homemade jam.

"We had a lot of hand-me-downs," Nephi said. "We got a big family. There was 10 of us and we had an old saying, 'First up, best dressed!' And you sure didn't want to be late for the breakfast table."

For family vacations, the Waymans did a lot of camping and fishing. "We weren't world travelers," Nephi said. "We did our traveling locally and just had a lot of fun. We always had people coming over to help and we'd play a lot of farm football."

"We didn't have a lot of the things that other kids had, but I never regretted a minute of it, because we had so much fun and so much love."

"All the things that we saw other kids suffering from," Nephi said, "broken families, money or not, they struggled while we had it good."

School was the one part of Nephi's life he didn't appreciate and enjoy. He never did very well at school.

"I'm not very smart by nature," He said. "So I had a hard time in school even though I made friends easily. I always looked forward to recess— that was my favorite part. I kept looking out the window wishing I was outside. "

"I had a lot of friends. Played a lot of sports. But I didn't like the academic part. That was very difficult for me."

In truth, Nephi detested school. So much so, he dropped out in the eighth grade. "I was always quite industrious," he said. "When I was about 12, I started earning money doing various odd jobs; mowing lawns, digging ditches, yard care for neighbors, all that kind of stuff. So I figured, *wrongly,* who needs school when I could be out there getting my hands dirty and earning money? So I skipped high school, which was a mistake," Nephi said.

Nephi's first real job, other than the odd jobs such as digging ditches, was driving a truck— a big flatbed diesel truck.

"We delivered supplies to plumbers," Nephi said. "Taps and water heaters, piping, all things 'plumbish.' I didn't have a car yet, so I'd ride my bike to work and then I'd get in this truck, 33 feet long. Big. Like a dump truck only flat."

"I was making $4.25 an hour. They made $16.25. So, I asked the obvious question, 'What does it take to be a plumber?' And this tough construction site plumber— his bumper sticker said *Number*

One In the Number Two Business — told me there were just three things to know."

"Crap goes downhill. We get paid on Fridays (because if they got paid on Tuesday, they take their paychecks to a bar and not show up to work for the rest of the week). And, 'Never bite your finger nails.' I decided I was going to be a plumber."

What the kid who despised school wasn't told was he'd have to go through four years of apprenticeship including college level math to get his plumber's license.

Remarkably — although he admits plumber's school was the hardest thing he'd ever done — Nephi aced it with a 4.0 grade-point average, and he did it while working full-time and helping on the farm every day. He amazed even himself.

"By the time I was 20," Nephi said, "I was a licensed technician with a truck, and doing heating and cooling repairs, too. I kind of had a baby face, so I would show up at Mrs. Jones' to fix her broken air conditioner and she'd look behind me to see if anybody else was coming. She thought I was the helper. I had to grow some whiskers, so they would trust me to work on their stuff."

Over the years, Nephi became a master of plumbing, heating and air conditioning trades — and many others as well. His specialized knowledge and varied experience was so extensive, he was hired by the government to oversee all of the maintenance on Federal buildings. A position he still maintains to this day.

Not for the money, which Nephi no longer needs, but because it brings

**him a constant flow of new people
he can help through his Youngevity
business.**

Nephi discovered Youngevity in fine plumber fashion. "I was on
my way to fix a broken toilet," he said. "I made up for my lack of
education by listening to the talk shows in my truck. This guy on
the radio said, 'A day without a hamburger is like a day without
sunshine.' I was shocked, because I was driving down the road
eating a hamburger! Of course if you asked any so-called health
expert at the time, nobody said anything good about burgers and
this doctor says you should eat one every day. So, I listened."

"People were calling in asking questions. The first one was a lady
asking about allergies and hay fever. My wife had suffered with
this for 20 years— *really* suffered. She couldn't even go outdoors
during the summer. She couldn't breathe, sinus headaches, really,
really terrible. And this doc says, 'Oh no problem.'"

"He rattles off a list of nutritional supplements and minerals for
her to take," Nephi said. "And I'm thinking this guy is either a
dang liar or he knows something all those doctors for 20 years
don't know. We had spent tens-of-thousands of dollars and been
to every medical expert there was trying to solve my wife's
problem."

**"To make the long story short, Dr.
Wallach says 'I'm in town tonight
doing a live lecture. It's free. Come
and listen.'"**

"So I go home and tell my wife and she's not the least thrilled
(she'd heard it all a thousand times before) until I told her the
hamburger story. Then she says, 'We should go listen to him.' So,
we went."

144

Nephi's wife loved Dr. Wallach right away. Nephi liked him too, because Doc grew up on a farm and Nephi knew from his own experience that what he was saying about the animals was true: You have to give them the proper nutrition to maintain their health, so you'd have a profitable farm. Dr. Wallach said the same was true for people. That made perfect sense to Nephi.

It took about six weeks to solve the problem Nephi's wife had for 20 years.

Nephi didn't know there was a business involved. He'd only listened to the *Dead Doctors Don't Lie* cassette he'd been given when he bought his products at that first meeting. He got some more to hand out because he felt strongly it was a message people had to hear.

"The next thing I know," Nephi said, "I get a check in the mail for $3. I thought it was some scam, so I threw it in the trash." By that time, they'd run out of products, but he didn't have the $150 to order more. Then Nephi got another check. It was for $50. Nephi called Jerry, the man he bought the products from, and asked what it was all about."

Jerry explained that Nephi had been sending people to them who'd ordered products and that was his "Thank you money" from the company. Nephi wondered what it would take to add another zero to that "Thank you." He was already working two jobs and his wife worked, as well. He was driving a 26 year-old Buick and had $120,000 in credit card debt. But he *had to* get money for more products.

Nephi started his business doing what he was already doing; lending people the *Dead Doctors...* tape,

because "They had to hear it."

All he wanted was to earn enough to pay for products for his wife. That happened in less than two months. In six months, Nephi's wife was able to quit the job she hated as a "visiting maid." Nephi was able to leave plumbing for a living within two years with his "Thank you money" from Youngevity.

"I'm a social guy," Nephi said. "I like people. In just a few minutes of conversation, people will tell you what bothers them. They'll speak about their circumstances, and I just try to stay alert and listen and see if there's a way I can help them. If I believe there is, I just ask them something like, 'Are you open to an idea?' It just happens. People order products. People join the business. And it happens and happens— and continues to happen."

"In this business of Youngevity," Nephi said, "you have to believe the message. You have to live it, breathe it and believe it in your core. It's a whole lot more than making money. It's a lot more than being healthy. It's the message of who Dr. Wallach is and what he's trying to accomplish."

"If people really saw what we could do we could save this country. We could save the entire financial system," Nephi said. "And in the process, flush a lot of rotten and corrupt things down the toilet in the medical system and the current so called healthcare system."

Spoken from the unique perspective of a plumber.

"We have an opportunity to fight against what I see as a takeover from the elite, dishonest people in government, and unethical people in general who want to control us," Nephi said.

"We give people options to change their circumstances. This is not

**rocket science. It's not impossible.
I'm living proof."**

"And if you do that with enough people, think of what we could accomplish; think of what we could change."

"Think of the hope we could give to families, people who don't see a way out of the rat race and the hole they're in. That's what gets me up and straps my boots on every day. Being able to know I can pull people up. I can show them the way out and give them hope."

And For Nephi Wayman, "That changes everything."

Nephi Wayman and his wife Joanie are life-long residents of the Salt Lake City area, where they live with their children Frances19, Jesssica 18, Emma 16, Kenneth 14, Joan Vilate 12, Matthais 10, Faith 5 and Hope who's 1. Nephi wants another child. You can guess what her name will be...

Last Words

Youngevity:
Paradigm Pioneers

Steve Wallach, CEO and Co-Founder of Youngevity (along with his wife Michelle, long-time partner Richard Renton and his father, Dr. Joel Wallach) has an aptitude for science. Quite understandable given how he grew up and *who* he grew up around.

"One of the tenets of science that has been ingrained in me," Steve said, "is to be observational."

"You have to always be looking— and what you see is a paradigm."

"I learned about the idea of *paradigms* from the book, *The Structure of Scientific Revolutions,* by Thomas Kuhn. If you look up the word in the dictionary," Steve said, "it means a model, a pattern, the design. I speak of a paradigm simply as *the way we think it is.*"

To illustrate, Steve tells the story of the Swiss watch.

Soon after the first pocket watch was down-sized and put on a strap to become the "Watch Wristlet" in the 1890s, the Swiss became the leading maker of the new personal, portable time pieces. The Swiss watch was *the* paradigm of wristwatches, and remained so for more than 70 years.

In the mid-1960s a research laboratory in Switzerland discovered quartz crystal technology. It was more accurate, smaller, lighter, and cheaper. As well, all of the mechanical challenges inherent with mainsprings, balance wheels, gears and 17 jewel movements no longer existed, so it kept working much longer as well.

But because the Swiss were so fully invested in their paradigm they had no interest in changing. After all, they already *owned* the watch business.

The quartz technology that was developed by the Swiss was picked up by Japanese manufacturer Seiko, and in less than a decade the quartz watch— "Made in Japan"— was the new paradigm of wristwatches throughout the world.

"The Swiss invented quartz technology," Steve explained. "They *shifted* the paradigm. But the Japanese were the ones who *pioneered* the new paradigm. They took it out of the lab, into the world — and they took it to the bank."

When you think of an affordable, accurate wrist watch today, what comes to mind? A Japanese quartz watch.

Dr. Joel Wallach, shifted the paradigm of the medical establishment's treatment of disease with surgery and drugs. He did that with a "radical" common sense approach of diet and nutrition that he presented in his mega-best-selling lecture and book, *Dead Doctors Don't Lie*.

Now, through the Youngevity family of companies, Steve and his father together are *pioneering a* new paradigm of the business of Health & Wellness in the 21st Century.

"One of the things about science," Steve said, "is that the greatest discoveries are what you *weren't* looking for. I've simply applied that to our business." That is, Youngevity was not what the Wallach's were *looking* for.

Prior to starting Youngevity, Steve, Michelle, Doc and their 10's-of-thousands of loyal consumers and business partners found themselves involved with a company that was swamped with personal and professional problems. The company was *supposed* to be making products made to Dr. Wallach's exacting specifications, shipping them, and paying people commissions for the sales they'd made— none of which was happening. They were *not* supposed to be siphoning-off millions of their people's well-earned dollars into foreign bank accounts, which was happening.

However, "My father is loyal to a fault," Steve said. "He was determined to solve the company's problems. He took responsibility for all that was wrong— and darn near *everything* was wrong— even though he had nothing to do with causing any of it."

But even Dr. Wallach's formidable skills and tireless efforts couldn't fix the nightmare the company had created.

If ever a business enterprise was born in the crucible of adversity— and blessed by Providence as well— it's Youngevity.

Someday the full Youngevity Story will be told. Not here. Not now. That's a book for another time. And although it will be a non-fiction book, most people probably won't believe it.

"Truth is stranger than fiction..." Mark Twain wrote, then added, "...but I am measurably familiar with it." So is Steve Wallach.

"If you can take something that's great for one thing and apply it to something completely different," Steve said, "all of a sudden you may have something new that's super exciting. I believe that's what we are doing with Youngevity."

Like another business pioneer who shares his first name, Steve Wallach is revolutionizing the business model of Network Marketing.

"When Steve Jobs started Apple Computers, that's what they were— computers," Steve said. "When we started Youngevity, we simply wanted to make my father's essential nutrition products right— what we now call "90 For Life." We also wanted to take care of our people. We were distributors, too. We knew what it took to honor and support the men and women in the field with integrity."

"Over time," Steve said, "Apple Computers rose above simply offering the best computers to become a company with the best technology. Now they're 'just' Apple, doing what Steve Jobs set out to do, 'To give people what they want— even when they don't know they want it.'"

"Nobody was banging on Apple's door demanding an iPod with iTunes or iPhones or iPads." Steve said. "Apple focused on using their core expertise to make people's lives better, giving them superior information, communication and entertainment products they didn't even know existed."

"That's what we're doing in Youngevity, only instead of technology, our expertise is Health and Wellness."

With 90 For Life as the hub, Youngevity has created and ever-expanding array of spokes— a select collection of diverse companies, each with one-of-a-kind lines that lead their individual product categories— supporting and strengthening the wheel of Health & Wellness.

The result is fulfilling Steve Wallach's vision of a "Generational Legacy Company."

Most people are familiar with five and 10 year goals, but 100 year goals? Rare indeed, and by some people's standards, even a bit crazy. That's not Steve Wallach's paradigm.

Influenced by his father who asserts that with a proper diet and the 90 essential nutrients all animals require, living in optimal health to 100 and beyond is the way life should be, Steve has once again transferred a concept from one domain to another: From long life to longevity in business.

"It goes back to the very beginning of starting the company," Steve said. "We were determined to do whatever it takes – and more – to be a company that lasts generations, to be a legacy company."

"Youngevity will continue to grow and evolve as a company. We're publicly traded (YGYI), so our people can benefit from ownership in the company. We're giving back to the global community with the *Be the Change* Foundation. We will expand further internationally, reaching more people throughout the world with the opportunity to transform their Health & Wellness, and acquire the lifestyle of Time, Freedom & Wealth they desire, dream of and deserve."

"I value this quote from Dag Hammarskjöld that pretty much says it all about Youngevity," Steve said.

"For all that has been— Thanks. For all that shall be— Yes!"

Each of the Network Marketers in this book became successful – very successful... millionaires.

There are many thousands just like them in this business all around the world.

Most of the people who read this book will not become millionaires.

But some of you... the ones that read the book again and again... those who read until the stories become part of you... you will begin to think and feel and act like The Greatest Networkers in the World.

Remember their clear message:

"If we can do it, so can you."

That's the good news.

The bad news is: Now you have no more excuses.

It will take time. It will take effort. You have to learn the skills. You have to work on yourself. And you cannot quit. But do those things and you will become successful — perhaps very successful, maybe even a millionaire.

Network Marketing will transform your life.

Let me know what I can do to help.

The Possibilities

Now you've met twenty-one of *The Greatest Networkers in the World.* Please know that there are many more within Youngevity. We couldn't fit them all in this book. Also please know — you could be one of them.

And now, you've learned that Network Marketing works when you work it. We hope you're convinced that remarkable success is possible for you, too, in Youngevity; no matter your age, sex, education, family background, past failures or successes. These true stories prove that.

On the back cover we told you that each of the twenty-one *Greatest Networkers* in this book had a message for you:

"If we can do it, so can you."

What we didn't tell you is that they *all* will help you do it.

Unlike any other business, Network Marketing is about people-helping-people. One simple reason that's true is because of the way we are paid. The more people we help achieve Health, Time and Money, the more we earn ourselves. It's more than fair. It's brilliant!

Something else you should know: Unlike most other Networking Companies, in Youngevity it doesn't matter who enrolled you, what particular team you're on, how or when you got involved, everybody helps everybody here.

Youngevity is a family. Not simply of many different companies, which we are, Youngevity is a growing global Network welcoming you everywhere you go; like family.

Please, think back over the stories you've read...

Was there anyone in the book like you?

Anybody here who was once where you are in your life right now?

Did you meet anyone in this book who is achieving the things you desire, dream of and deserve?

We say we're in the Health & Wellness business, but that's not the whole story.

Youngevity transforms people's lives. That's our real business.

If you're ready to transform your life for the better, forever... Reconnect with the person who turned you on to this book. He or she will be happy to listen to any questions or concerns you have. You'll find us to be curious and candid: We want to learn who and how you are, and you can count on honest and sincere answers to any of your questions.

Our goal is not to "get" you as a customer or a business partner. The people in Youngevity are looking for a fit — what's the highest good for you and for all concerned.

We are passionate about the Mission we share with our Founder, Dr. Joel Wallach:

To help people achieve all the Health and Wealth that's truly possible for them.

Now you know, those possibilities are yours....